THE WORKS 7

Brian Moses left teaching in 1988 to write full time. Since then he has written and edited over 170 books, including *Behind the Staffroom Door: The Very Best of Brian Moses* (also available on CD) and the picture book *The Snake Hotel* (both Macmillan). He is also a performance poet and percussionist who has read his poems in a multitude of schools and libraries throughout the UK. He also undertakes residencies at international schools in Europe. Brian lives in a tiny village in Sussex with his wife Anne, their daughters Karen and Linette, a brood of bad-tempered chickens, a rabbit and an extremely loopy labrador called Honey.

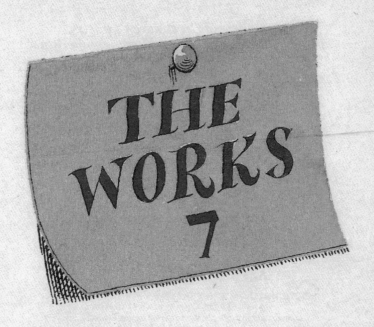

THE WORKS 7

Classic poems for the literacy hour

Chosen by Brian Moses

MACMILLAN CHILDREN'S BOOKS

For my friends in children's poetry,
and in children's poetry publishing; inheritors
of a grand tradition, without which . . .

and with thanks to Rachel Maconachy.

First published 2008 by Macmillan Children's Books
a division of Macmillan Publishers Limited
20 New Wharf Road, London N1 9RR
Basingstoke and Oxford
www.panmacmillan.com

Associated companies throughout the world

ISBN 978-0-330-44424-8

1 3 5 7 9 8 6 4 2

A CIP catalogue record for this book is available from
the British Library.

Print Kent

Contents

Contents

Time

Travel and Places

Contents

Night

Weather

Contents

Seasons

The Sea

Contents

Creatures

Contents

People

Contents

Conflict

Magic and Mystery

Contents

Colours

Nonsense Poems

Modern Classics

Contents

Introduction

What a wonderful invitation! Fill a big fat book with classic poems, poems written many years ago that have stood the test of time and still say something to us today. What an opportunity to cram all of my favourite poems into one volume.

I have to admit that I hated poetry at school and I didn't understand much of it! I think probably because so much of it was treated unimaginatively in the classroom.

Now, many years later, I think differently. I began to appreciate William Wordsworth while visiting the Lake District and seeing what he saw as I read his poems. A friend took William Blake's poem *London* and turned it into a song. I was intrigued, read more and learned about Blake's life. A teaching colleague and I took Browning's *The Pied Piper of Hamelin* and turned it into a stage show for our classes to perform. I found Gustave Doré's wonderfully imaginative illustrations for *The Rime of the Ancient Mariner* and was fascinated by what he'd conjured up from the text.

Sometimes it was simply hearing an Oscar-winning rendition of a poem that did it for me. I was hooked on the rhythms and the rhymes, on wonderful choruses that I couldn't shift from my head. Gradually I began to love the poetry I had rejected as a teenager.

As a teacher, I also started to realize that there is a wealth of material from the past that is accessible, and can be introduced to children in ways which foster enjoyment and understanding.

Introduction

It is important, we know, that children do hear and see all kinds of poetry and with this in mind I have tried to select poems from a great tradition which will capture both hearts and minds. In many instances the whole poem is included but at other times, for example with *The Rhyme of the Ancient Mariner*, I have quoted extracts which will hopefully fire the imagination.

Both *Kubla Khan* and *The Pied Piper of Hamelin* tell of fantastic lands, and few children will fail to be captured by the opening verse of the former or intrigued by the notion of a sunny pleasure-dome with caves of ice!

Other poems invite us to speculate about a mystery. Why does the traveller never return to the shore in Longfellow's *The Tide Rises, the Tide Falls*? Where is the traveller heading on the darkest evening of the year in Robert Frost's *Stopping by Woods on a Snowy Evening*? And in *The Listeners* by Walter de la Mare, who is the horseman, why is he knocking on the moonlit door, and did he ever return?

Although written many years ago, a number of poems are about subjects which will be only too familiar to children today. Who hasn't gone to bed on a summer's evening when it's still light outside and been unable to sleep? It happened to Robert Louis Stevenson too. William Blake wondered why he had to go to school on a hot summer's day when there were far more interesting things that he could be doing. W. B. Yeats writes about a place to escape to in *The Lake Isle of Innisfree* and in Rudyard Kipling's *The Way Through the Woods*, he writes about something he liked to do but which is now denied him.

Knowing something about the background to a poem can

reveal more about the poem and why it was composed. When did *The Charge of the Light Brigade* take place and what caused it? A knowledge of highwaymen will be useful when reading about *The Highwayman* and his love for Bess, the landlord's black-eyed daughter. Longfellow grew up by the sea and his understanding of its great power was reflected in poems such as *The Wreck of the Hesperus*. Wordsworth's *Composed Upon Westminster Bridge, 1802* still resonates for anyone standing in that same position over two hundred years later.

In the last section of the book I have allowed myself to predict what will be the modern classics, which poems will last and will be reprinted in poetry anthologies many years into the future.

Some of the poems included here work best in a one-to-one relationship. Nothing else is needed save the child, the poem and the imaginative pull. Others will come over best through a powerful performance from a teacher or visiting writer. Some may work as group presentations, or with a musical background. I have given a few more examples as to how poems may be presented at the back of this book.

Finally, any choice is subjective and there will be favourites that I've missed. So make this anthology organic, add your choices, because in the final analysis the poems you like the best will be the ones for which you feel the most. You will pass on your love for, and enjoyment of, these pieces to those who encounter them with you.

Brian Moses

Childhood

from *Rock Me to Sleep*

Backward, turn backward, O Time, in your flight,
Make me a child again just for tonight! . . .

Elizabeth Akers Allen

I Remember, I Remember

I remember, I remember,
    The house where I was born,
The little window where the sun
    Came peeping in at morn;
He never came a wink too soon,
    Nor brought too long a day,
But now, I often wish the night
    Had borne my breath away.

I remember, I remember,
    The roses, red and white;
The violets, and the lily-cups,
    Those flowers made of light!
The lilacs where the robin built,
    And where my brother set
The laburnum on his birthday –
    The tree is living yet!

I remember, I remember,
　　Where I was used to swing;
And thought the air must rush as fresh
　　To swallows on the wing:
My spirit flew in feathers then,
　　That is so heavy now,
And summer pools could hardly cool
　　The fever on my brow!

I remember, I remember,
　　The fir trees dark and high;
I used to think their slender tops
　　Were close against the sky:
It was a childish ignorance,
　　But now 'tis little joy
To know I'm farther off from Heav'n
　　Than when I was a boy.

Thomas Hood

There Was a Child Went Forth

There was a child went forth every day;
And the first object he looked upon, that object he became.
And that object became part of him for the day, or a
    certain part of the day, or for many years, or stretching
    cycles of years:
The early lilacs became part of this child . . .
And the apple-trees covered with blossoms, and the fruit
    afterward, and wood-berries, and the commonest weeds
    by the road;
And the schoolmistress that passed on her way to the
    school . . .

The blow, the quick loud word, the tight bargain, the
    crafty lure,
The family usages, the language, the company, the
    furniture – the yearning and swelling heart . . .

The doubts of day-time and the doubts of night-time – the
    curious whether and how,
Whether that which appears is so, or is it all flashes and
    specks?
Men and women crowding fast in the streets – if they are
    not flashes and specks, what are they?

These became part of that child who went forth every day,
    and who now goes, and will always go forth every day.

Walt Whitman

The Land of Story-Books

At evening when the lamp is lit,
Around the fire my parents sit;
They sit at home and talk and sing,
And do not play at anything.

Now, with my little gun, I crawl
All in the dark along the wall,
And follow round the forest track
Away behind the sofa back.

There, in the night, where none can spy,
All in my hunter's camp I lie,
And play at books that I have read
Till it is time to go to bed.

These are the hills, these are the woods,
These are my starry solitudes;
And there the river by whose brink
The roaring lions come to drink.

I see the others far away
As if in firelit camp they lay,
And I, like to an Indian scout,
Around their party prowled about.

So, when my nurse comes in for me,
Home I return across the sea,
And go to bed with backward looks
At my dear land of Story-books.

Robert Louis Stevenson

I Wish I Were

When the gong sounds at ten in the morning and I walk
  to school by our lane,
Every day I meet the hawker crying, 'Bangles, crystal
  bangles!'
There is nothing to hurry him on, there is no road he must
  take, no place he must go to, no time when he must
  come home.
I wish I were a hawker, spending my day in the road,
  crying, 'Bangles, crystal bangles!'

When at four in the afternoon I come back from the school,
I can see through the gate of that house the gardener
  digging the ground.
He does what he likes with his spade, he soils his clothes
  with the dust,
Nobody takes him to task if he gets baked in the sun or
  gets wet.
I wish I were a gardener digging away at the garden with
  nobody to stop me from digging.

Just as it gets dark in the evening and my mother sends me
    to bed,
I can see through my open window the watchman walking
    up and down.
The lane is dark and lonely, and the street-lamp stands
Like a giant with one red eye in its head.

The watchman swings his lantern and walks with his
    shadow at his side, and never once goes to bed in his
    life.
I wish I were a watchman walking the streets all night,
    chasing the shadows with my lantern.

Rabindranath Tagore

If I Knew

If I knew the box where the smiles are kept,
No matter how large the key,
Or strong the bolt I would try so hard
'Twould open I know for me,
Then over the land and sea broadcast
I'd scatter the smiles to play,
That the children's faces might hold them fast
For many and many a day.

If I knew the box that was large enough
To hold all the frowns I meet,
I would like to gather them every one
From the nursery, school or street,
Then, folding and holding, I'd pack them in
And turning the monster key,
I'd hire a giant to drop the box
To the depths of the deep, deep sea.

Anon.

My Shadow

I have a little shadow that goes in and out with me,
And what can be the use of him is more than I can see.
He is very, very like me from the heels up to the head;
And I see him jump before me, when I jump into my bed.

The funniest thing about him is the way he likes to grow –
Not at all like proper children, which is always very slow;
For he sometimes shoots up taller like an India rubber ball,
And he sometimes gets so little that there's none of him at
   all.

He hasn't got a notion of how children ought to play,
And can only make a fool of me in every sort of way.
He stays so close beside me, he's a coward you can see;
I'd think shame to stick to nursie as that shadow sticks to
    me!

One morning, very early, before the sun was up,
I rose and found the shining dew on every buttercup;
But my lazy little shadow, like an arrant sleepy-head,
Had stayed at home behind me and was fast asleep in bed.

Robert Louis Stevenson

The School Boy

I love to rise in a summer morn
When the birds sing on every tree;
The distant huntsman winds his horn,
And the sky-lark sings with me:
O, what sweet company!

But to go to school in a summer morn,
O! it drives all joy away;
Under a cruel eye outworn
The little ones spend the day
In sighing and dismay.

Ah! then at times I drooping sit,
And spend many an anxious hour;
Nor in my book can I take delight,
Nor sit in learning's bower,
Worn through with the dreary shower.

How can the bird that is born for joy
Sit in a cage and sing?
How can a child when fears annoy
But droop his tender wing,
And forget his youthful spring?

O! Father and Mother, if buds are nipped,
And blossoms blown away,
And if the tender plants are stripped
Of their joy in the springing day
By sorrow and care's dismay,

How shall the summer arise in joy
Or the summer fruits appear?
Or how shall we gather what griefs destroy
Or bless the mellowing year,
When the blasts of winter appear?

William Blake

The Children's Hour

Between the dark and the daylight,
    When the light is beginning to lower,
Comes a pause in the day's occupations
    That is known as the Children's Hour.

I hear in the chamber above me
    The patter of little feet,
The sound of a door that is opened,
    And voices soft and sweet.

From my study I see in the lamplight,
    Descending the broad hall stair,
Grave Alice and laughing Allegra,
    And Edith with golden hair.

A whisper, and then a silence;
    Yet I know by their merry eyes,
They are plotting and planning together
    To take me by surprise.

A sudden rush from the stairway,
    A sudden raid from the hall!
By three doors left unguarded
    They enter my castle wall!

They climb up into my turret,
    O'er the arms and back of my chair;
If I try to escape, they surround me;
    They seem to be everywhere.

They almost devour me with kisses,
    Their arms about me entwine,
Till I think of the Bishop of Bingen
    In his Mouse-Tower on the Rhine.

Do you think, O blue-eyed banditti,
    Because you have scaled the wall,
Such an old mustache as I am
    Is not a match for you all?

I have you fast in my fortress,
    And will not let you depart,
But put you down into the dungeon
    In the round-tower of my heart.

And there will I keep you forever,
    Yes, forever and a day,
Till the wall shall crumble to ruin,
    And moulder in dust away.

Henry Wadsworth Longfellow

Big and Little Things

I cannot do the big things
  That I should like to do,
To make the earth for ever fair,
  The sky for ever blue.

But I can do the small things
  That help to make it sweet,
Though clouds arise and fill the skies,
  And tempests beat.

I cannot stay the raindrops
  That tumble from the skies;
But I can wipe the tears away
  From baby's pretty eyes.

I cannot make the sun shine,
  Or warm the winter bleak;
But I can make the summer come
  On sister's rosy cheek.

I cannot stay the storm clouds,
  Or drive them from their place;
But I can clear the clouds away
  From brother's troubled face.

Childhood

I cannot make the corn grow,
Or work upon the land;
But I can put new strength and will
In father's busy hand.

I cannot stay the east wind,
Or thaw its icy smart;
But I can keep a corner warm
In mother's loving heart.

I cannot do the big things
That I should like to do,
To make the earth for ever fair,
The sky for ever blue.

But I can do the small things
That help to make it sweet,
Though clouds arise and fill the skies
And tempests beat.

Alfred H. Miles

Children

If children live with criticism
they learn to condemn

If children live with hostility
they learn to fight

If children live with ridicule
   they learn to be shy

If children live with shame
   they learn to feel guilty

If children live with tolerance
   they learn to be patient

If children live with encouragement
   they learn confidence

If children live with praise
   they learn to appreciate

If children live with fairness
   they learn justice

If children live with security
   they learn to have faith

If children live with approval
   they learn to like themselves

If children live with acceptance and friendship
   they learn to find love in the world

Anon.

Farewell to the Farm

The coach is at the door at last;
The eager children, mounting fast
And kissing hands, in chorus sing:
Good-bye, good-bye, to everything!

To house and garden, field and lawn,
The meadow-gates we swang upon,
To pump and stable, tree and swing,
Good-bye, good-bye, to everything!

And fare you well for evermore,
O ladder at the hayloft door,
O hayloft where the cobwebs cling,
Good-bye, good-bye, to everything!

Crack goes the whip, and off we go;
The trees and houses smaller grow;
Last, round the woody turn we swing:
Good-bye, good-bye, to everything!

Robert Louis Stevenson

To Any Reader

As from the house your mother sees
You playing round the garden trees,
So you may see, if you will look
Through the windows of this book,
Another child, far, far away,
And in another garden, play.
But do not think you can at all,
By knocking on the window, call
That child to hear you. He intent
Is all on his play-business bent.
He does not hear; he will not look,
Nor yet be lured out of his book.
For, long ago, the truth to say,
He has grown up and gone away,
And it is but a child of air
That lingers in the garden there.

Robert Louis Stevenson

A Good Play

We built a ship upon the stairs
All made of the back-bedroom chairs,
And filled it full of sofa pillows
To go a-sailing on the billows.

We took a saw and several nails,
And water in the nursery pails;
And Tom said, 'Let us also take
An apple and a slice of cake';
Which was enough for Tom and me
To go a-sailing on, till tea.

We sailed along for days and days,
And had the very best of plays;
But Tom fell out and hurt his knee,
So there was no one left but me.

Robert Louis Stevenson

Daddy Fell into the Pond

Everyone grumbled. The sky was gray.
We had nothing to do and nothing to say.
We were nearing the end of a dismal day,
And there seemed to be nothing beyond,
  THEN
  Daddy fell into the pond!

And everyone's face grew merry and bright,
And Timothy danced for sheer delight.
'Give me the camera, quick, oh quick!
He's crawling out of the duckweed.' *Click!*

Then the gardener suddenly slapped his knee,
And doubled up, shaking silently,
And the ducks all quacked as if they were daft
And it sounded as if the old drake laughed.

Oh, there wasn't a thing that didn't respond
   WHEN
   Daddy fell into the pond!

            Alfred Noyes

Allie

'Allie, call the birds in,
The birds from the sky.'
Allie calls, Allie sings,
Down they all fly.
First there came
Two white doves,
Then a sparrow from his nest,
Then a clucking bantam hen,
Then a robin red-breast.

Childhood

'Allie, call the beasts in,
The beasts, every one.'
Allie calls, Allie sings,
In they all run.
First there came
Two black lambs,
Then a grunting Berkshire sow,
Then a dog without a tail,
Then a red and white cow.

'Allie, call the fish up,
The fish from the stream.'
Allie calls, Allie sings,
Up they all swim.
First there came
Two gold fish,
A minnow and a miller's thumb,
Then a pair of loving trout,
Then the twisting eels come.

'Allie, call the children
Children from the green.'
Allie calls, Allie sings,
Soon they run in.
First there came
Tom and Madge
Kate and I who'll not forget
How we played by the water's edge
Till the April sun set.

Robert Graves

21

A Boy's Song

Where the pools are bright and deep,
Where the grey trout lies asleep,
Up the river and over the lea,
That's the way for Billy and me.

Where the blackbird sings the latest,
Where the hawthorn blooms the sweetest,
Where the nestlings chirp and flee,
That's the way for Billy and me.

Where the mowers mow the cleanest,
Where the hay lies thick and greenest,
There to track the homeward bee,
That's the way for Billy and me.

Where the hazel bank is steepest,
Where the shadow falls the deepest,
Where the clustering nuts fall free,
That's the way for Billy and me.

Why the boys should drive away
Little sweet maidens from the play,
Or love to banter and fight so well,
That's the thing I never could tell.

But this I know, I love to play
Through the meadow, among the hay;
Up the water and over the lea,
That's the way for Billy and me.

James Hogg

Child Labour

'For oh,' say the children, 'we are weary
And we cannot run or leap;
If we care for any meadows, it were merely
To drop down in them and sleep.
Our knees tremble sorely in the stooping,
We fall upon our faces, trying to go;
And underneath our heavy eyelids drooping
The reddest flower would look as pale as snow.
For, all day, we drag our burden tiring
Through the coal-dark, underground;
Or, all day, we drive the wheels of iron
In the factories, round and round.

For all day the wheels are droning, turning;
Their wind comes in our faces,
Till our hearts turn, our heads with pulses burning,
And the walls turn in their places:
Turns the long light that drops adown the wall,
Turn the black flies that crawl along the ceiling:

All are turning, all the day, and we with all.
And all day, the iron wheels are droning,
And sometimes we could pray,
'O ye wheels' (breaking out in mad moaning)
'Stop! Be silent for today!'

Elizabeth Barrett Browning

The Chimney Sweeper

When my mother died I was very young,
And my father sold me while yet my tongue
Could scarcely cry ''weep! 'weep! 'weep! 'weep!'
So your chimneys I sweep, and in soot I sleep.

There's little Tom Dacre, who cried when his head,
That curled like a lamb's back, was shaved: so I said
'Hush, Tom! never mind it, for when your head's bare
You know that the soot cannot spoil your white hair.'

And so he was quiet, and that very night,
As Tom was a-sleeping, he had such a sight!
That thousands of sweepers, Dick, Joe, Ned, and Jack,
Were all of them locked up in coffins of black.

And by came an Angel who had a bright key,
And he opened the coffins and set them all free;
Then down a green plain leaping, laughing, they run,
And wash in a river, and shine in the Sun.

Then naked and white, all their bags left behind,
They rise upon clouds and sport in the wind;
And the Angel told Tom, if he'd be a good boy,
He'd have God for his father, and never want joy.

And so Tom awoke; and we rose in the dark,
And got with our bags and our brushes to work.
Tho' the morning was cold, Tom was happy and warm;
So if all do their duty they need not fear harm.

William Blake

Hiawatha's Childhood

By the shores of Gitche Gumee,
By the shining Big-Sea-Water,
Stood the wigwam of Nokomis,
Daughter of the Moon, Nokomis.
Dark behind it rose the forest,
Rose the black and gloomy pine-trees,
Rose the firs with cones upon them;
Bright before it beat the water,
Beat the clear and sunny water,
Beat the shining Big-Sea-Water.
    There the wrinkled old Nokomis
Nursed the little Hiawatha,
Rocked him in his linden cradle,
Bedded soft in moss and rushes,

Safely bound with reindeer sinews;
Stilled his fretful wail by saying,
'Hush! the Naked Bear will hear thee!'
Lulled him into slumber, singing,
'Ewa-yea! my little owlet!'
Who is this, that lights the wigwam?
With his great eyes lights the wigwam?
Ewa-yea! my little owlet!'
   Many things Nokomis taught him
Of the stars that shine in heaven;
Showed him Ishkoodah, the comet,
Ishkoodah, with fiery tresses;
Showed the Death-Dance of the spirits,
Warriors with their plumes and war-clubs,
Flaring far away to northward
In the frosty nights of winter;
Showed the broad white road in heaven,
Pathway of the ghosts, the shadows,
Running straight across the heavens,
Crowded with the ghosts, the shadows.
   At the door on summer evenings,
Sat the little Hiawatha;
Heard the whispering of the pine-trees,
Heard the lapping of the waters,
Sounds of music, words of wonder;
'Minne-wawa!' said the pine-trees,
'Mudway-aushka!' said the water.
   Saw the fire-fly Wah-wah-taysee,
Flitting through the dusk of evening,
With the twinkle of its candle

26

Lighting up the brakes and bushes,
And he sang the song of children,
Sang the song Nokomis taught him:
'Wah-wah-taysee, little fire-fly,
Little, flitting, white-fire insect,
Little, dancing, white-fire creature,
Light me with your little candle,
Ere upon my bed I lay me,
Ere in sleep I close my eyelids!'

Saw the moon rise from the water,
Rippling, rounding from the water,
Saw the flecks and shadows on it,
Whispered, 'What is that, Nokomis?'
And the good Nokomis answered:
'Once a warrior, very angry,
Seized his grandmother, and threw her
Up into the sky at midnight;
Right against the moon he threw her;
'Tis her body that you see there.'

Saw the rainbow in the heaven,
In the eastern sky the rainbow,
Whispered, 'What is that, Nokomis?'
And the good Nokomis answered:
''Tis the heaven of flowers you see there;
All the wild-flowers of the forest,
All the lilies of the prairie,
When on earth they fade and perish,
Blossom in that heaven above us.'

When he heard the owls at midnight,
Hooting, laughing in the forest,

'What is that?' he cried in terror;
'What is that,' he said, 'Nokomis?'
And the good Nokomis answered:
'That is but the owl and owlet,
Talking in their native language,
Talking, scolding at each other.'
    Then the little Hiawatha
Learned of every bird its language,
Learned their names and all their secrets,
How they built their nests in summer,
Where they hid themselves in winter,
Talked with them whene'er he met them,
Called them 'Hiawatha's Chickens.'
    Of all beasts he learned the language,
Learned their names and all their secrets,
How the beavers built their lodges,
Where the squirrels hid their acorns,
How the reindeer ran so swiftly,
Why the rabbit was so timid,
Talked with them whene'er he met them,
Called them 'Hiawatha's Brothers.'

Henry Wadsworth Longfellow

If

If you can keep your head when all about you
   Are losing theirs and blaming it on you;
If you can trust yourself when all men doubt you,
   But make allowance for their doubting too:
If you can wait and not be tired by waiting,
   Or, being lied about, don't deal in lies,
Or being hated don't give way to hating,
   And yet don't look too good, nor talk too wise;

If you can dream – and not make dreams your master;
   If you can think – and not make thoughts your aim,
If you can meet with Triumph and Disaster
   And treat those two impostors just the same:
If you can bear to hear the truth you've spoken
   Twisted by knaves to make a trap for fools,
Or watch the things you gave your life to, broken,
   And stoop and build 'em up with worn-out tools;

If you can make one heap of all your winnings
   And risk it on one turn of pitch-and-toss,
And lose, and start again at your beginnings,
   And never breathe a word about your loss:
If you can force your heart and nerve and sinew
   To serve your turn long after they are gone,
And so hold on when there is nothing in you
   Except the Will which says to them: 'Hold on!'

If you can talk with crowds and keep your virtue,
   Or walk with Kings – nor lose the common touch,
If neither foes nor loving friends can hurt you,
   If all men count with you, but none too much:
If you can fill the unforgiving minute
   With sixty seconds' worth of distance run,
Yours is the Earth and everything that's in it,
   And – which is more – you'll be a Man, my son!

Rudyard Kipling

My Mother Said

My mother said, I never should
Play with gypsies in the wood.

If I did, then she would say:
'Naughty girl to disobey!

'Your hair shan't curl and your shoes shan't shine,
You gypsy girl, you shan't be mine!'

And my father said that if I did,
He'd rap my head with the teapot-lid.

My mother said that I never should
Play with the gypsies in the wood.

The wood was dark, the grass was green;
By came Sally with a tambourine.

I went to sea – no ship to get across;
I paid ten shillings for a blind white horse.

I upped on his back and was off in a crack,
Sally tell my mother I shall never come back.

Anon.

Time

from *As You Like It*
Act II scene vii

All the world's a stage,
And all the men and women merely players;
They have their exits and their entrances,
And one man in his time plays many parts,
His acts being seven ages. At first the infant,
Mewling and puking in the nurse's arms:
And then the whining schoolboy, creeping like snail
Unwillingly to school. And then the lover,
Sighing like furnace, with a woeful ballad
Made to his mistress' eyebrow. Then, a soldier,
Full of strange oaths, and bearded like the pard,
Jealous in honour, sudden and quick in quarrel,
Seeking the bubble reputation
Even in the cannon's mouth. And then, the justice,
In fair round belly, with good capon lin'd,
With eyes severe and beard of formal cut,
Full of wise saws, and modern instances,
And so he plays his part. The sixth age shifts
Into the lean and slipper'd pantaloon,
With spectacles on nose, and pouch on side,
His youthful hose well sav'd, a world too wide
For his shrunk shank; and his big manly voice,
Turning again toward childish treble, pipes
And whistles in his sound. Last scene of all,
That ends this strange eventful history,
Is second childishness and mere oblivion;
Sans teeth, sans eyes, sans taste, sans every thing.

William Shakespeare

How Many?

How many seconds in a minute?
Sixty, and no more in it.

How many minutes in an hour?
Sixty for sun and shower.

How many hours in a day?
Twenty-four for work and play.

How many days in a week?
Seven both to hear and speak.

How many weeks in a month?
Four, as the swift moon runn'th.

How many months in a year?
Twelve the almanack makes clear.

How many years in an age?
One hundred says the sage.

How many ages in time?
No one knows the rhyme.

Christina Rossetti

Ecclesiastes 3:1–9

To everything there is a season, and a time to every
purpose under heaven.
A time to be born, and a time to die.
A time to plant, and a time to pluck up what is planted.
A time to kill, and a time to heal.
A time to break down, and a time to build up.
A time to weep and a time to laugh.
A time to mourn, and a time to dance.
A time to cast away stones, and a time to gather stones
together.
A time to embrace, and a time to refrain from embracing.
A time to seek, and a time to lose.
A time to keep, and a time to cast away.
A time to rend, and a time to sew.
A time to keep silence, and a time to speak.
A time to love, and a time to hate.
A time of war, and a time of peace.

King James Bible

Haroun Al Raschid

One day, Haroun Al Raschid read
A book wherein the poet said: –

'Where are the kings, and where the rest
Of those who once the world possessed?

'They're gone with all their pomp and show,
They're gone the way that thou shalt go.

'O thou who choosest for thy share
The world, and what the world calls fair,

'Take all that it can give or lend,
But know that death is at the end!'

Haroun Al Raschid bowed his head:
Tears fell upon the page he read.

Henry Wadsworth Longfellow

from *Six Things for Christmas*

So, six things that once upon a time
I lost:
One: is a bald sad man I lost somewhere
Within my seventeenth year.
Two: was an acquaintance that I had with Mt Kerinyaga,
Whom I also loved.
Three: a parcel of thoughts that I continually lose.
Four: a mouse called Nuisance that was all grey.
Five: a beautiful Aunt who gave me a sight
Of two grey heron when I was a boy.
Six: that thing we all lost so long ago – Christmas.

John May

Nine-o'Clock Bell!

Nine-o'Clock Bell!
Nine-o'Clock Bell!
All the small children and big ones as well,
Pulling their socks up, snatching their hats,
Cheeking and grumbling and giving back-chats,
Laughing and quarrelling, dropping their things,
These at a snail's pace, and those upon wings,
Lagging behind a bit, running ahead,
Waiting at corners for lights to turn red,

Some of them scurrying,
Others not worrying,
Carelessly trudging or anxiously hurrying,
All through the streets they are coming pell-mell
At the Nine-o'Clock
Nine-o'Clock
Nine-o'Clock
Bell!

Eleanor Farjeon

I Stood on a Tower in the Wet

I stood on a tower in the wet,
And New Year and Old Year met,
And winds were roaring and blowing;
And I said, 'O years, that meet in tears,
Have ye aught that is worth the knowing?
Science enough and exploring,
Wanderers coming and going,
Matter enough for deploring,
But aught that is worth the knowing?'
Seas at my feet were flowing,
Waves on the shingle pouring,
Old Year roaring and blowing,
And New Year blowing and roaring.

Alfred, Lord Tennyson

Keepsake Mill

Over the borders, a sin without pardon,
Breaking the branches and crawling below,
Out through the breach in the wall of the garden,
Down by the banks of the river, we go.
Here is the mill with the humming of thunder,
Here is the weir with the wonder of foam,
Here is the sluice with the race running under –
Marvellous places, though handy to home!
Sounds of the village grow stiller and stiller,
Stiller the note of the birds on the hill;
Dusty and dim are the eyes of the miller,
Deaf are his ears with the moil of the mill.
Years may go by, and the wheel in the river
Wheel as it wheels for us, children, today,
Wheel and keep roaring and foaming for ever
Long after all of the boys are away.
Home from the Indies and home from the ocean,
Heroes and soldiers we all shall come home;
Still we shall find the old mill wheel in motion,
Turning and churning that river to foam.
You with the bean that I gave when we quarrelled,
I with your marble of Saturday last,
Honoured and old and all gaily apparelled,
Here we shall meet and remember the past.

Robert Louis Stevenson

The Way Through the Woods

They shut the road through the woods
Seventy years ago.
Weather and rain have undone it again,
And now you would never know
There was once a road through the woods
Before they planted the trees.
It is underneath the coppice and heath,
And the thin anemones.
Only the keeper sees
That, where the ring-dove broods,
And the badgers roll at ease,
There was once a road through the woods.

Yet, if you enter the woods
Of a summer evening late,
When the night-air cools on the trout-ringed pools
Where the otter whistles his mate
(They fear not men in the woods,
Because they see so few),
You will hear the beat of a horse's feet,
And the swish of a skirt in the dew,
Steadily cantering through
The misty solitudes,
As though they perfectly knew
The old lost road through the woods . . .
But there is no road through the woods!

Rudyard Kipling

Mother to Son

Well, son, I'll tell you:
Life for me ain't been no crystal stair.
It's had tacks in it,
And splinters,
And boards torn up,
And places with no carpet on the floor –
Bare.
But all the time
I'se been a-climbin' on,
And reachin' landin's,
And turnin' corners,
And sometimes goin' in the dark
Where there ain't been no light.
So, boy, don't you turn back.
Don't you set down on the steps
'Cause you find it kinder hard.
Don't you fall now –
For I'se still goin', honey,
I'se still climbin',
And life for me ain't been no crystal stair.

Langston Hughes

Remember

Remember me when I am gone away,
   Gone far away into the silent land;
   When you can no more hold me by the hand,
Nor I half turn to go yet turning stay.
Remember me when no more day by day
   You tell me of our future that you plann'd:
   Only remember me; you understand
It will be late to counsel then or pray.
Yet if you should forget me for a while
   And afterwards remember, do not grieve:
   For if the darkness and corruption leave
   A vestige of the thoughts that once I had,
Better by far you should forget and smile
   Than that you should remember and be sad.

Christina Rossetti

Travel and Places

The Key of the Kingdom

This is the Key of the Kingdom:
In that Kingdom there is a city;
In that city is a town;
In that town there is a street;
In that street there winds a lane;
In that lane there is a yard;
In that yard there is a house;
In that house there waits a room;
In that room an empty bed;
And on that bed a basket –
A basket of sweet flowers:
  Of flowers, of flowers;
  A basket of sweet flowers.

Flowers in a basket;
Basket on the bed;
Bed in the chamber;
Chamber in the house;
House in the weedy yard;
Yard in the winding lane;
Lane in the broad street;
Street in the high town;
Town in the city;
City in the Kingdom –
This is the Key of the Kingdom.
  Of the Kingdom this is the Key.

Anon.

Pleasant Sounds

The rustling of leaves under the feet in woods and under
  hedges;
The crumpling of cat-ice and snow down woodrides,
  narrow lanes and every street causeway;
Rustling through a wood or rather rushing, while the wind
  halloos in the oak-top like thunder;
The rustle of birds' wings startled from their nests or flying
  unseen into the bushes;
The whizzing of larger birds overheard in a wood, such as
  crows, puddocks, buzzards;

The trample of robins and woodlarks on the brown leaves,
  and the patter of squirrels on the green moss;
The fall of an acorn on the ground, the pattering of nuts
  on the hazel branches as they fall from ripeness;
The flirt of the ground-lark's wink from the stubbles – how
  sweet such pictures on dewy mornings, when the dew
  flashes from its brown feathers!

John Clare

Miracles

Why, who makes much of a miracle?
As to me I know of nothing else but miracles,
Whether I walk the streets of Manhattan,
Or dart my sight over the roofs of houses toward the sky,
Or wade with naked feet along the beach just in the edge
   of the water,
Or stand under trees in the woods,
Or talk by day with anyone I love, or sleep in the bed at
   night with anyone I love,
Or sit at table at dinner with the rest,
Or look at strangers opposite me riding in the car,
Or watch honey-bees busy around the hive of a summer
   fore-noon,
Or animals feeding in the fields,
Or birds, or the wonderfulness of insects in the air,
Or the wonderfulness of the sundown, or of stars shining
   so quiet and bright,
Or the exquisite delicate thin curve of the new moon in
   spring;
These with the rest, one and all, are to me miracles,
The whole referring, yet each distinct and in its place.
To me every hour of the light and dark is a miracle,
Every cubic inch of space is a miracle,
Every square yard of the surface of the earth is spread with
   the same,
Every foot of the interior swarms with the same.

To me the sea is a continual miracle,
The fishes that swim – the rocks – the motion of the
    waves – the ships with men in them,
What stranger miracles are there?

Walt Whitman

The Lake Isle of Innisfree

I will arise and go now, and go to Innisfree,
And a small cabin build there, of clay and wattles made:
Nine bean rows will I have there, a hive for the honey-bee,
    And live alone in the bee-loud glade.

And I shall have some peace there, for peace comes
    dropping slow,
Dropping from the veils of the morning to where the
    cricket sings;
There midnight's all a glimmer, and noon a purple glow,
    And evening full of the linnet's wings.

I will arise and go now, for always night and day
I hear lake water lapping with low sounds by the shore;
While I stand on the roadway, or on the pavements grey,
    I hear it in the deep heart's core.

W. B. Yeats

Ozymandias

I met a traveller from an antique land
Who said: Two vast and trunkless legs of stone
Stand in the desert . . . Near them, on the sand,
Half sunk, a shattered visage lies, whose frown,
And wrinkled lip, and sneer of cold command,
Tell that its sculptor well those passions read
Which yet survive, stamped on these lifeless things,
The hand that mocked them, and the heart that fed:
And on the pedestal these words appear:
'My name is Ozymandias, king of kings:
Look on my works, ye Mighty, and despair!'
Nothing beside remains. Round the decay
Of that colossal wreck, boundless and bare
The lone and level sands stretch far away.

Percy Bysshe Shelley

The Pedlar's Caravan

I wish I lived in a caravan,
With a horse to drive, like the pedlar-man!
Where he comes from nobody knows,
Or where he goes to, but on he goes!

His caravan has windows two,
And a chimney of tin, that the smoke comes through;
He has a wife, with a baby brown,
And they go riding from town to town.

Chairs to mend, and delf to sell!
He clashes the basins like a bell;
Tea-trays, baskets ranged in order,
Plates with the alphabet round the border!

The roads are brown, and the sea is green,
But his house is just like a bathing-machine;
The world is round, and he can ride,
Rumble and splash, to the other side!

With the pedlar-man I should like to roam,
And write a book when I came home;
All the people would read my book,
Just like the Travels of Captain Cook.

William Brighty Rands

How They Brought the Good News from Ghent to Aix

I sprang to the stirrup, and Joris, and he;
I galloped, Dirck galloped, we galloped all three;
'Good speed!' cried the watch, as the gate-bolts undrew;
'Speed!' echoed the wall to us galloping through;
Behind shut the postern, the lights sank to rest,
And into the midnight we galloped abreast.

Not a word to each other; we kept the great pace
Neck by neck, stride by stride, never changing our place;
I turned in my saddle and made its girths tight,
Then shortened each stirrup, and set the pique right,
Rebuckled the cheek-strap, chained slacker the bit,
Nor galloped less steadily Roland a whit.

'Twas moonset at starting; but while we drew near
Lokeren, the cocks crew and twilight dawned clear;
At Boom, a great yellow star came out to see;
At Duffeld, 'twas morning as plain as could be;
And from Mecheln church-steeple we heard the half-chime
So Joris broke silence with, 'Yet there is time!'

At Aerschot, up leaped of a sudden the sun,
And against him the cattle stood black every one,
To stare thro' the mist at us galloping past,
And I saw my stout galloper Roland at last,
With resolute shoulders, each butting away
The haze, as some bluff river headland its spray.

And his low head and crest, just one sharp ear bent back
For my voice, and the other pricked out on his track;
And one eye's black intelligence – ever that glance
O'er its white edge at me, his own master, askance!
And the thick heavy spume-flakes which aye and anon
His fierce lips shook upwards in galloping on.

By Hasselt, Dirck groaned; and, cried Joris, 'Stay spur!!
Your Roos galloped bravely, the fault's not in her,
We'll remember at Aix' – for one heard the quick wheeze
Of her chest, saw the stretched neck and staggering knees,
And sunk tail, and horrible heave of the flank,
As down on her haunches she shuddered and sank.

So we were left galloping, Joris and I,
Past Looz and past Tongres, no cloud in the sky;
The broad sun above laughed a pitiless laugh,
'Neath our feet broke the brittle bright stubble like chaff;
Till over by Dalhem a dome-spire sprang white,
And 'Gallop,' gasped Joris, 'for Aix is in sight!'

'How they'll greet us!' – and all in a moment his roan
Rolled neck and crop over, lay dead as a stone;
And there was my Roland to bear the whole weight
Of the news which alone could save Aix from her fate,
With his nostrils like pits full of blood to the brim,
And with circles of red for his eye-sockets' rim.

Then I cast loose my buffcoat, each holster let fall,
Shook off both my jack-boots, let go belt and all,
Stood up in the stirrup, leaned, patted his ear,
Called my Roland his pet-name, my horse without peer;
Clapped my hands, laughed and sang, any noise, bad or
   good,
Till at length into Aix Roland galloped and stood.

And all I remember is, friends flocking round
As I sat with his head 'twixt my knees on the ground;
And no voice but was praising this Roland of mine,
As I poured down his throat our last measure of wine,
Which (the burgesses voted by common consent)
Was no more than his due who brought good news from
   Ghent.

Robert Browning

From a Railway Carriage

Faster than fairies, faster than witches,
Bridges and houses, hedges and ditches;
And charging along like troops in a battle,
All through the meadows the horses and cattle:
All of the sights of the hill and the plain
Fly as thick as driving rain;
And ever again in the wink of an eye,
Painted stations whistle by.

Here is a child who clambers and scrambles,
All by himself and gathering brambles;
Here is a tramp who stands and gazes;
And there is the green for stringing the daisies!
Here is a cart run away in the road
Lumping along with man and load;
And here is a mill, and there is a river:
Each a glimpse and gone for ever!

Robert Louis Stevenson

Adlestrop

Yes. I remember Adlestrop –
The name, because one afternoon
Of heat the express-train drew up there
Unwontedly. It was late June.

The steam hissed. Someone cleared his throat.
No one left and no one came
On the bare platform. What I saw
Was Adlestrop – only the name

And willows, willow-herb, and grass,
And meadowsweet, and haycocks dry,
No whit less still and lonely fair
Than the high cloudlets in the sky.

And for that minute a blackbird sang
Close by, and round him, mistier,
Farther and farther, all the birds
Of Oxfordshire and Gloucestershire.

Edward Thomas

Stopping by Woods on a Snowy Evening

Whose woods these are I think I know.
His house is in the village though;
He will not see me stopping here
To watch his woods fill up with snow.

My little horse must think it queer
To stop without a farmhouse near
Between the woods and frozen lake
The darkest evening of the year.

He gives his harness bells a shake
To ask if there is some mistake.
The only other sound's the sweep
Of easy wind and downy flake.

The woods are lovely, dark and deep,
But I have promises to keep,
And miles to go before I sleep,
And miles to go before I sleep.

Robert Frost

My Heart's in the Highlands

My heart's in the Highlands, my heart is not here;
My heart's in the Highlands a-chasing the deer;
Chasing the wild deer, and following the roe;
My heart's in the Highlands, wherever I go.
Farewell to the Highlands, farewell to the North,
The birthplace of valour, the country of worth;
Wherever I wander, wherever I rove,
The hills of the Highlands for ever I love.

Farewell to the mountains, high-covered with snow;
Farewell to the straths and green valleys below;
Farewell to the forests and wild-hanging woods;
Farewell to the torrents and loud-pouring floods.
My heart's in the Highlands, my heart is not here;
My heart's in the Highlands a-chasing the deer;
Chasing the wild deer, and following the roe;
My heart's in the Highlands, wherever I go.

Robert Burns

Skye Boat Song

Sing me a song of a lad that is gone,
  Say, could that lad be I?
Merry of soul he sailed on a day
  Over the sea to Skye.

Mull was astern, Rum on the port,
    Eigg on the starboard bow;
Glory of youth glowed in his soul:
    Where is that glory now?

Sing me a song of a lad that is gone,
    Say, could that lad be I?
Merry of soul he sailed on a day
    Over the sea to Skye.

Give me again all that was there,
    Give me the sun that shone!
Give me the eyes, give me the soul,
    Give me the lad that's gone!

Sing me a song of a lad that is gone,
    Say, could that lad be I?
Merry of soul he sailed on a day
    Over the sea to Skye.

Billow and breeze, islands and seas,
    Mountains of rain and sun,
All that was good, all that was fair,
    All that was me is gone.

Robert Louis Stevenson

Composed upon Westminster Bridge, 1802

Earth has not anything to show more fair:
Dull would he be of soul who could pass by
A sight so touching in its majesty:
This City now doth, like a garment, wear
The beauty of the morning; silent, bare,
Ships, towers, domes, theatres, and temples lie
Open unto the fields, and to the sky;
All bright and glittering in the smokeless air
Never did sun more beautifully steep
In his first splendour, valley, rock, or hill;
Ne'er saw I, never felt, a calm so deep!
The river glided at his own sweet will:
Dear God! the very houses seem asleep;
And all that mighty heart is lying still!

William Wordsworth

Mannahatta

I was asking for something specific and perfect for my city,
Whereupon lo! upsprang the aboriginal name.
Now I see what there is in a name, a word, liquid, sane,
   unruly, musical, self-sufficient,

I see that the word of my city is that word from of old,

Because I see that word nested in nests of water-bays, superb,

Rich, hemm'd thick all around with sailships and steamships, an island sixteen miles long, solid-founded.

Numberless crowded streets, high growths of iron, slender, strong, light, splendidly uprising toward clear skies,

Tides swift and ample, well-loved by me, toward sundown,

The flowing sea-currents, the little islands, larger adjoining islands, the heights, the villas,

The countless masts, the white shore-steamers, the lighters, the ferry-boats, the black sea-steamers, well-model'd,

The down-town streets, the jobbers' houses of business, the houses of business of the ship-merchants and money-brokers, the river-streets,

Immigrants arriving, fifteen or twenty thousand in a week,

The carts hauling goods, the manly race of drivers of horses, the brown-faced sailors,

The summer air, the bright sun shining, and the sailing clouds aloft,

The winter snows, the sleigh-bells, the broken ice in the river, passing along up or down with the flood-tide or ebb-tide,

The mechanics of the city, the masters, well-form'd, beautiful-faced, looking you straight in the eyes,

Trottoirs throng'd, vehicles, Broadway, the women, the shops and shows,

A million people – manners free and superb – open voices – hospitality – the most courageous and friendly young men,

City of hurried and sparkling waters! city of spires and
   masts!
City nested in bays! my city!

Walt Whitman

from *The Cataract of Lodore*

The Cataract strong
Then plunges along,
Striking and raging
As if a war waging
Its caverns and rocks among:
Rising and leaping,
Sinking and creeping,
Swelling and sweeping,
Showering and springing,
Flying and flinging,
Writhing and ringing,
Eddying and whisking,
Spouting and frisking,
Turning and twisting,
Around and around
With endless rebound!
Smiting and fighting,
A sight to delight in;
Confounding, astounding,
Dizzying and deafening the ear with its sound.

Robert Southey

Inversnaid

This darksome burn, horseback brown,
His rollrock highroad roaring down,
In coop and in comb the fleece of his foam
Flutes and low to the lake falls home.

A windpuff-bonnet of fawn-froth
Turns and twindles over the broth
Of a pool so pitchblack, fell-frowning,
It rounds and rounds Despair to drowning.

Degged with dew, dappled with dew
Are the groins of the braes that the brook treads through,
Wiry heathpacks, flitches of fern,
And the beadbonny ash that sits over the burn.

What would the world be, once bereft
Of wet and of wildness? Let them be left,
O let them be left, wildness and wet;
Long live the weeds and the wilderness yet.

Gerard Manley Hopkins

Where Go the Boats?

Dark brown is the river,
    Golden is the sand.
It flows along for ever,
    With trees on either hand.

Green leaves a-floating,
    Castles of the foam,
Boats of mine a-boating –
    Where will all come home?

On goes the river,
    And out past the mill,
Away down the valley,
    Away down the hill.

Away down the river,
    A hundred miles or more,
Other little children
    Shall bring my boats ashore.

Robert Louis Stevenson

Up-Hill

Does the road wind up-hill all the way?
　Yes, to the very end.
Will the day's journey take the whole long day?
　From morn to night, my friend.

But is there for the night a resting-place?
　A roof for when the slow dark hours begin.
May not the darkness hide it from my face?
　You cannot miss that inn.

Shall I meet other wayfarers at night?
　Those who have gone before.
Then must I knock, or call when just in sight?
　They will not keep you standing at that door.

Shall I find comfort, travel-sore and weak?
　Of labour you shall find the sum.
Will there be beds for me and all who seek?
　Yea, beds for all who come.

Christina Rossetti

Evening: Ponte al Mare, Pisa

The sun is set; the swallows are asleep;
  The bats are flitting fast in the grey air;
The slow soft toads out of damp corners creep,
  And evening's breath, wandering here and there
Over the quivering surface of the stream,
Wakes not one ripple from its summer dream.

There is no dew on the dry grass tonight,
  Nor damp within the shadow of the trees;
The wind is intermitting, dry, and light;
  And in the inconstant motion of the breeze
The dust and straws are driven up and down,
And whirled about the pavement of the town.

Within the surface of the fleeting river
  The wrinkled image of the city lay,
Immovably unquiet, and for ever
  It trembles, but it never fades away . . .

Percy Bysshe Shelley

At the Railway Station, Upway

'There is not much that I can do,
  For I've no money that's quite my own!'
  Spoke up the pitying child –
A little boy with a violin
At the station before the train came in –
'But I can play my fiddle to you,
And a nice one 'tis, and good in tone!'

  The man in the handcuffs smiled;
The constable looked, and he smiled, too,
  As the fiddle began to twang;
And the man in the handcuffs suddenly sang
        With grimful glee:
        'This life so free
        Is the thing for me!'
And the constable smiled, and said no word,
As if unconscious of what he heard;
And so they went on till the train came in –
The convict, and boy with the violin.

Thomas Hardy

The Brook

I come from haunts of coot and hern,
I make a sudden sally,
And sparkle out among the fern,
To bicker down a valley.

By thirty hills I hurry down,
Or slip between the ridges,
By twenty thorps, a little town,
And half a hundred bridges.

Till last by Philip's farm I flow
To join the brimming river,
For men may come and men may go,
But I go on for ever.

I chatter over stony ways,
In little sharps and trebles,
I bubble into eddying bays,
I babble on the pebbles.

With many a curve my banks I fret
By many a field and fallow,
And many a fairy foreland set
With willow-weed and mallow.

I chatter, chatter, as I flow
To join the brimming river,
For men may come and men may go,
But I go on for ever.

I wind about, and in and out
With here a blossom sailing,
And here and there a lusty trout,
And here and there a grayling,

And here and there a foamy flake
Upon me, as I travel
With many a silvery waterbreak
Above the golden gravel,

And draw them all along, and flow
To join the brimming river,
For men may come and men may go,
But I go on for ever.

I steal by lawns and grassy plots,
I slide by hazel covers;
I move the sweet forget-me-nots
That grow for happy lovers.

I slip, I slide, I gloom, I glance,
Among my skimming swallows;
I make the netted sunbeam dance
Against my sandy shallows.

I murmur under moon and stars
In brambly wildernesses;
I linger by my shingly bars;
I loiter round my cresses;

And out again I curve and flow
To join the brimming river,
For men may come and men may go,
But I go on for ever.

Alfred, Lord Tennyson

Night

Village Before Sunset

There is a moment country children know
When half across the field the shadows go
And even the birds sing leisurely and slow.

There's timelessness in every passing tread;
Even the far-off train as it puffs ahead,
Even the voices calling them to bed.

Frances Cornford

The Lamplighter

My tea is nearly ready and the sun has left the sky.
It's time to take the window to see Leerie going by;
For every night at teatime and before you take your seat,
With lantern and with ladder he comes posting up the street.
Now Tom would be a driver and Maria go to sea,
And my papa's a banker and as rich as he can be;
But I, when I am stronger and can choose what I'm to do,
O Leerie, I'll go round at night and light the lamps with you!
For we are very lucky, with a lamp before the door,
And Leerie stops to light it as he lights so many more;
And oh! before you hurry by with ladder and with light;
O Leerie, see a little child and nod to him tonight!

Robert Louis Stevenson

Bed in Summer

In winter I get up at night
And dress by yellow candle-light.
In summer quite the other way
I have to go to bed by day.

I have to go to bed and see
The birds still hopping on the tree,
Or hear the grown-up people's feet
Still going past me in the street.

And does it not seem hard to you,
When all the sky is clear and blue,
And I should like so much to play,
To have to go to bed by day?

Robert Louis Stevenson

Escape at Bedtime

The lights from the parlour and kitchen shone out
  Through the blinds and the windows and bars;
And high overhead and all moving about,
  There were thousands of millions of stars.
There ne'er were such thousands of leaves on a tree,
  Nor people in church or the park,

As the crowds of the stars that looked down upon me,
 And that glittered and winked in the dark.
The Dog, and the Plough, and the Hunter, and all,
 And the star of the sailor, and Mars.
These shone in the sky, and the pail by the wall
 Would be half full of water and stars.
They saw me at last, and they chased me with cries,
 And they soon had me packed into bed;
But the glory kept shining and bright in my eyes,
 And the stars going round in my head.

Robert Louis Stevenson

Night-Lights

There is no need to light a night-light
On a light night like tonight;
For a night-light's light's a slight light
When the moonlight's white and bright.

Anon.

75

The Moon

The moon has a face like the clock in the hall;
She shines on thieves on the garden wall,
On streets and fields and harbour quays,
And birdies asleep in the forks of the trees.

The squalling cat and the squeaking mouse,
The howling dog by the door of the house,
The bat that lies in bed at noon,
All love to be out by the light of the moon.

But all of the things that belong to the day
Cuddle to sleep to be out of her way;
And flowers and children close their eyes
Till up in the morning the sun shall arise.

Robert Louis Stevenson

The Night Mail

This is the night mail crossing the border,
Bringing the cheque and the postal order,
Letters for the rich, letters for the poor,
The shop at the corner and the girl next door,
Pulling up Beattock, a steady climb –
The gradient's against her but she's on time.

Past cotton grass and moorland boulder,
Shovelling white steam over her shoulder,
Snorting noisily as she passes
Silent miles of wind-bent grasses;
Birds turn their heads as she approaches,
Stare from the bushes at her blank-faced coaches;
Sheepdogs cannot turn her course,
They slumber on with paws across;
In the farm she passes no one wakes
But a jug in a bedroom gently shakes.

Dawn freshens, the climb is done.
Down towards Glasgow she descends
Towards the steam tugs, yelping down the glade of cranes
Towards the fields of apparatus, the furnaces
Set on the dark plain like gigantic chessmen.
All Scotland waits for her;
In the dark glens, beside the pale-green sea lochs,
Men long for news.

Letters of thanks, letters from banks,
Letters of joy from the girl and boy,
Receipted bills and invitations
To inspect new stock or visit relations,
And applications for situations,
And timid lovers' declarations,
And gossip, gossip from all the nations,
News circumstantial, news financial,
Letters with holiday snaps to enlarge in,
Letters with faces scrawled on the margin.

Letters from uncles, cousins and aunts,
Letters to Scotland from the South of France,
Letters of condolence to Highlands and Lowlands,
Notes from overseas to the Hebrides;
Written on paper of every hue,
The pink, the violet, the white and the blue,
The chatty, the catty, the boring, adoring,
The cold and official and the heart's outpouring,
Clever, stupid, short and long,
The typed and the printed and the spelt all wrong.

Thousands are still asleep
Dreaming of terrifying monsters
Or a friendly tea beside the band at Cranston's or
   Crawford's;
Asleep in working Glasgow, asleep in well-set Edinburgh,
Asleep in granite Aberdeen.
They continue their dreams
But shall wake soon and long for letters.
And none will hear the postman's knock
Without a quickening of the heart,
For who can bear to feel himself forgotten?

W. H. Auden

An August Midnight

I

A shaded lamp and a waving blind,
And the beat of a clock from a distant floor:
On this scene enter – winged, horned, and spined –
A longlegs, a moth, and a dumbledore;
While 'mid my page there idly stands
A sleepy fly, that rubs its hands . . .

II

Thus meet we five, in this still place,
At this point of time, at this point in space.
– My guests besmear my new-penned line,
Or bang at the lamp and fall supine.
'God's humblest, they!' I muse. Yet why?
They know Earth-secrets that know not I.

Thomas Hardy

So We'll Go No More A Roving

So, we'll go no more a roving
    So late into the night,
Though the heart be still as loving,
    And the moon be still as bright.

For the sword outwears its sheath,
   And the soul wears out the breast,
And the heart must pause to breathe,
   And love itself have rest.

Though the night was made for loving,
   And the day returns too soon,
Yet we'll go no more a roving
   By the light of the moon.

Lord Byron

The Night Will Never Stay

The night will never stay,
The night will still go by,
Though with a million stars
You pin it to the sky;
Though you bind it with the blowing wind
And buckle it with the moon,
The night will slip away
Like sorrow or a tune.

Eleanor Farjeon

Will There Really Be a 'Morning'?

Will there really be a 'Morning'?
Is there such a thing as 'Day'?
Could I see it from the mountains
If I were as tall as they?

Has it feet like Water lilies?
Has it feathers like a Bird?
Is it brought from famous countries
Of which I have never heard?

Oh, some Scholar! Oh, some Sailor!
Oh, some Wise Man from the skies!
Please to tell a little Pilgrim
Where the place called 'Morning' lies!

Emily Dickinson

Is the Moon Tired?

Is the moon tired? She looks so pale
    Within her misty veil;
She scales the sky from east to west,
    And takes no rest.

Before the coming of the night
   The moon shows papery white;
Before the dawning of the day
   She fades away.

Christina Rossetti

The Early Morning

The moon on the one hand, the dawn on the other:
The moon is my sister, the dawn is my brother.
The moon on my left hand and the dawn on my right.
My brother, good morning: my sister, good night.

Hilaire Belloc

Weather

Whether

Whether the weather be fine
Or whether the weather be not
Whether the weather be cold
Or whether the weather be hot –
We'll weather the weather
Whatever the weather
Whether we like it or not!

Anon.

Weathers

This is the weather the cuckoo likes,
   And so do I;
When showers betumble the chestnut spikes,
   And nestlings fly;
And the little brown nightingale bills his best,
And they sit outside at 'The Travellers' Rest',
And maids come forth sprig-muslin drest,
And citizens dream of the south and west,
   And so do I.

This is the weather the shepherd shuns.
   And so do I;
When beeches drip in browns and duns,
   And thresh, and ply;
And hill-hid tides throb, throe on throe,
And meadow rivulets overflow,
And drops on gate-bars hang in a row,
And rooks in families homeward go,
   And so do I.

Thomas Hardy

Rain in Summer

How beautiful is the rain!
After the dust and the heat,
In the broad and fiery street,
In the narrow lane,
How beautiful is the rain!

How it clatters along the roofs
Like the tramp of hoofs,
How it gushes and struggles out
From the throat of the overflowing spout!

Across the window-pane
It pours and pours;
And swift and wide,
With a muddy tide,
Like a river down the gutter roars
The rain, the welcome rain!

Henry Wadsworth Longfellow

Didn't It Rain

Now, didn't it rain, chillun,
God's gonna 'stroy this world with water,
Now didn't it rain, my Lord,
Now didn't it rain, rain, rain.

Well, it rained forty days and it rained forty nights,
There wasn't no land nowhere in sight,
God sent a raven to carry the news,
He histe his wings and away he flew.

Well, it rained forty days and forty nights without
stopping,
Noah was glad when the rain stopped-a-dropping.
God sent Noah a rainbow sign,
Says, 'No more water, but fire next time.'

They knocked at the window and they knocked at the
   door.
They cried, 'O Noah, please take me on board.'
Noah cried, 'You're full of sin,
The Lord's got the key and you can't get in.'

Anon.

The Rainy Day

The day is cold, and dark, and dreary;
It rains, and the wind is never weary;
The vine still clings to the mouldering wall,
But at every gust the dead leaves fall,
And the day is dark and dreary.

My life is cold, and dark, and dreary;
It rains, and the wind is never weary;
My thoughts still cling to the mouldering Past,
But the hopes of youth fall thick in the blast,
And the days are dark and dreary.

Be still, sad heart! And cease repining;
Behind the clouds is the sun still shining;
Thy fate is the common fate of all,
Into each life some rain must fall,
Some days must be dark and dreary.

Henry Wadsworth Longfellow

Windy Nights

Whenever the moon and stars are set,
   Whenever the wind is high,
All night long in the dark and wet,
   A man goes riding by.
Late in the night when the fires are out,
Why does he gallop and gallop about?

Whenever the trees are crying aloud,
   And ships are tossed at sea,
By, on the highway, low and loud,
   By at the gallop goes he.
But at the gallop he goes, and then
By he comes back at the gallop again.

Robert Louis Stevenson

Who Has Seen the Wind?

Who has seen the wind?
   Neither I nor you:
But when the leaves hang trembling
   The wind is passing through.

Who has seen the wind?
Neither you nor I:
But when the trees bow down their heads
The wind is passing by.

Christina Rossetti

The North Wind Doth Blow

The north wind doth blow
And we shall have snow,
And what will poor robin do then, poor thing?
  He'll sit in a barn,
  And keep himself warm,
And hide his head under his wing, poor thing!

The north wind doth blow
And we shall have snow,
And what will the dormouse do then, poor thing?
  Roll'd up like a ball,
  In his nest snug and small,
He'll sleep till warm weather comes in, poor thing!

The north wind doth blow
And we shall have snow,
And what will the children do then, poor things?
  When lessons are done,
  They must skip, jump, and run,
Until they have made themselves warm, poor things!

Anon.

The Leaves in a Frolic

The leaves had a wonderful frolic,
  They danced to the wind's loud song,
They whirled, and they floated, and scampered,
  They circled and flew along.

The moon saw the little leaves dancing,
  Each looked like a small brown bird.
The man in the moon smiled and listened,
  And this is the song he heard.

The North Wind is calling, is calling,
  And we must whirl round and round,
And when our dancing is ended
  We'll make a warm quilt for the ground.

Anon.

The Snowman

Once there was a snowman
Stood outside the door,
Thought he'd like to come inside
And run around the floor;
Though he'd like to warm himself
By the firelight red;
Thought he'd like to clamber up
On that big white bed.
So he called the North Wind, 'Help me now I pray.
I'm completely frozen, standing here all day.'
So the North Wind came along and blew him in the door –
And now there's nothing left of him
But a puddle on the floor.

Anon.

Snow

In the gloom of whiteness,
In the great silence of snow,
A child was sighing
And bitterly saying: 'Oh,
They have killed a white bird up there on her nest.
The down is fluttering from her breast!'
And still it fell through that dusky brightness
On the child crying for the bird of the snow.

Edward Thomas

Snow in the Suburbs

Every branch big with it,
    Bent every twig with it;
  Every fork like a white web-foot;
  Every street and pavement mute:
Some flakes have lost their way, and grope back upward,
    when
Meeting those meandering down they turn and descend
    again.
    The palings are glued together like a wall,
    And there is no waft of wind with the fleecy fall.

    A sparrow enters the tree,
        Whereon immediately
A snow-lump thrice his own slight size
Descends on him and showers his head and eyes,
        And overturns him,
        And near inurns him,
    And lights on a nether twig, when its brush
Starts off a volley of other lodging lumps with a rush.

    The steps are a blanched slope,
        Up which, with feeble hope,
A black cat comes, wide-eyed and thin;
        And we take him in.

Thomas Hardy

Seasons

The Months of the Year

January brings the snow;
Makes the toes and fingers glow.

February brings the rain,
Thaws the frozen ponds again.

March brings breezes loud and shrill,
Stirs the dancing daffodil.

April brings the primrose sweet,
Scatters daisies at our feet.

May brings flocks of pretty lambs,
Skipping by their fleecy dams.

June brings tulips, lilies, roses;
Fills the children's hands with posies.

Hot July brings cooling showers,
Strawberries and gilly-flowers.

August brings the sheaves of corn,
Then the Harvest home is borne.

Warm September brings the fruit,
Sportsmen then begin to shoot.

Fresh October brings the pheasant;
Then to gather nuts is pleasant.

Dull November brings the blast,
Then the leaves are falling fast.

Chill December brings the sleet,
Blazing fire and Christmas treat.

Sara Coleridge

The Months

January cold desolate;
February all dripping wet;
March wind ranges;
April changes;
Birds sing in tune
   To flowers of May,
And sunny June
   Brings longest day;
In scorched July
The storm-clouds fly;
Lightning-torn
August bears corn.
September fruit;
In rough October

Earth must disrobe her;
Stars fall and shoot
In keen November;
And night is long
And cold is strong
In bleak December.

Christina Rossetti

The New Year

The Young New Year has come so soon
I wonder where the Old Years go?
To some dim land behind the moon
Where starlight glimmers, pale and low.

And everything is grey and cold
And there they sit, those ancient years,
Their eyes so kind, and dim and old
Their faces lined with vanished cares.

Their voices rattle, dry like bones,
The while they talk of what has been,
And murmur in their hollow tones
Of all the triumphs they have seen.

While the Young Year, with earnest eyes,
Comes buoyant on, to run his race,
Nor dreams how fast his life-span flies
Nor how his end draws on apace.

Anon.

A Change in the Year

It is the first mild day of March:
   Each minute sweeter than before,
The redbreast sings from the tall larch
   That stands beside our door.

There is a blessing in the air,
   Which seems a sense of joy to yield
To the bare trees, and mountains bare;
   And grass in the green field.

William Wordsworth

Daffodils

I wandered lonely as a cloud
That floats on high o'er vales and hills,
When all at once I saw a crowd,
A host, of golden daffodils;
Beside the lake, beneath the trees,
Fluttering and dancing in the breeze.

Continuous as the stars that shine
And twinkle on the Milky Way,
They stretched in never-ending line
Along the margin of a bay:
Ten thousand saw I at a glance,
Tossing their heads in sprightly dance.

The waves beside them danced, but they
Out-did the sparkling waves in glee:
A poet could not but be gay,
In such a jocund company:
I gazed – and gazed – but little thought
What wealth the show to me had brought.

For oft, when on my couch I lie
In vacant or in pensive mood,
They flash upon that inward eye
Which is the bliss of solitude;
And then my heart with pleasure fills,
And dances with the daffodils.

William Wordsworth

In the Summer

In the summer when I go to bed
The sun still streaming overhead
My bed becomes so small and hot
With sheets and pillow in a knot,
And then I lie and try to see
The things I'd really like to be.

I think I'd be a glossy cat
A little plump, but not too fat.
I'd never touch a bird or mouse
I'm much too busy round the house.

And then a fierce and hungry hound
The king of dogs for miles around;
I'd chase the postman just for fun
To see how quickly he could run.

Perhaps I'd be a crocodile
Within the marshes of the Nile
And paddle in the river-bed
With dripping mud-caps on my head.

Or maybe next a mountain goat
With shaggy whiskers at my throat,
Leaping streams and jumping rocks
In stripey pink and purple socks.

Or else I'd be a polar bear
And on an iceberg make my lair;
I'd keep a shop in Baffin Sound
To sell icebergs by the pound.

And then I'd be a wise old frog
Squatting on a sunken log,
I'd teach the fishes lots of games
And how to read and write their names.

An Indian lion then I'd be
And lounge about on my settee;
I'd feed on nothing but bananas
And spend all day in my pyjamas.

I'd like to be a tall giraffe
making lots of people laugh,
I'd do a tap dance in the street
with little bells upon my feet.

And then I'd be a foxy fox
Streaking through the hollyhocks,
Horse or hound would ne'er catch me
I'm a master of disguise, you see.

I think I'd be a chimpanzee
With musical ability,
I'd play a silver clarinet
Or form a Monkey String Quartet.

And then a snake with scales of gold
Guarding hoards of wealth untold,
No thief would dare to steal a pin –
But friends of mine I would let in.

But then before I really know
Just what I'd be or where I'd go
My bed becomes so wide and deep
And all my thoughts are fast asleep.

Thomas Hood

Fly Away, Fly Away

Fly away, fly away over the sea,
Sun-loving swallow, for summer is done;
Come again, come again, come back to me,
Bringing the summer and bringing the sun.

Christina Rossetti

Something Told the Wild Geese

Something told the wild geese
It was time to go,
Though the fields lay golden
Something whispered, 'Snow!'
Leaves were green and stirring,
Berries lustre-glossed,
But beneath warm feathers
Something cautioned, 'Frost!'

All the sagging orchards
Steamed with amber spice,
But each wild beast stiffened
At remembered ice.
Something told the wild geese
It was time to fly –
Summer sun was on their wings,
Winter in their cry.

Rachel Field

Guy Fawkes

Remember, remember
The fifth of November,
Gunpowder, treason and plot;
I see no reason
Why gunpowder treason
Should ever be forgot.

Anon.

No!

No sun – no moon!
No morn – no noon –
No dawn – no dusk – no proper time of day –
No sky – no earthly view –
No distance looking blue –
No road – no street – no 't'other side the way' –
No end to any Row –
No indications where the Crescents go –
No top to any steeple –
No recognitions of familiar people –
No courtesies for showing 'em –
No knowing 'em! –
No travelling at all – no locomotion,
No inkling of the way – no notion –
'No go' – by land or ocean –
No mail – no post –

No news from any foreign coast –
No Park – no Ring – no afternoon gentility –
  No company – no nobility –
No warmth, no cheerfulness, no healthful ease,
No comfortable feel in any member –
No shade, no shine, no butterflies, no bees,
No fruits, no flowers, no leaves, no birds –
  November!

Thomas Hood

Sheep in Winter

The sheep get up and make their many tracks
And bear a load of snow upon their backs,
And gnaw the frozen turnip to the ground
With sharp quick bite, and then go noising round
The boy that pecks the turnips all the day
And knocks his hands to keep the cold away
And laps his legs in straw to keep them warm
And hides behind the hedges from the storm.
The sheep, as tame as dogs, go where he goes
And try to shake their fleeces from the snows,
Then leave their frozen meal and wander round
The stubble stack that stands beside the ground,
And lie all night and face the drizzling storm
And shun the hovel where they might be warm.

John Clare

A Christmas Carol

In the bleak mid-winter
   Frosty wind made moan,
Earth stood hard as iron,
   Water like a stone;
Snow had fallen, snow on snow,
   Snow on snow,
In the bleak mid-winter
   Long ago.

Our God, heaven cannot hold Him,
   Nor earth sustain;
Heaven and earth shall flee away
   When He comes to reign:
In the bleak mid-winter
   A stable-place sufficed
The Lord God Almighty,
   Jesus Christ.

What can I give him,
   Poor as I am?
If I were a shepherd
   I would bring a lamb;
If I were a wise man
   I would do my part –
Yet what I can, I give Him,
   Give my heart.

Christina Rossetti

A Visit from St Nicholas

'Twas the night before Christmas, when all through the
　house
Not a creature was stirring, not even a mouse;
The stockings were hung by the chimney with care,
In hopes that St Nicholas soon would be there;
The children were nestled all snug in their beds,
While visions of sugar-plums danced in their heads;
And Mamma in her 'kerchief and I in my cap,
Had just settled our brains for a long winter's nap –
When out on the lawn there arose such a clatter,
I sprang from my bed to see what was the matter.
Away to the window I flew like a flash,
Tore open the shutters, and threw up the sash.
The moon, on the breast of the new-fallen snow,
Gave the lustre of midday to objects below;
When, what to my wondering eyes should appear,
But a miniature sleigh and eight tiny reindeer,
With a little old driver, so lively and quick,
I knew in a moment it must be St Nick.
More rapid than eagles his coursers they came,
And he whistled, and shouted, and called them by name:
'Now, *Dasher*! now, *Dancer*! now, *Prancer* and *Vixen*!
On, *Comet*! on, *Cupid*! on, *Donder* and *Blitzen*!
To the top of the porch! to the top of the wall!
Now dash away! dash away! dash away all!'
As dry leaves that before the wild hurricane fly,
When they meet with an obstacle, mount to the sky;
So up to the house-top the coursers they flew

With the sleigh full of toys, and St Nicholas too.
And then, in a twinkling, I heard on the roof
The prancing and pawing of each little hoof –
As I drew in my head, and was turning around,
Down the chimney St Nicholas came with a bound.
He was dressed all in fur, from his head to his foot,
And his clothes were all tarnished with ashes and soot;
A bundle of toys he had flung on his back,
And he looked like a pedlar just opening his pack.
His eyes – how they twinkled; his dimples, how merry!
His cheeks were like roses, his nose like a cherry!
His droll little mouth was drawn up like a bow,
And the beard of his chin was as white as the snow;
The stump of a pipe he held tight in his teeth,
And the smoke it encircled his head like a wreath;
He had a broad face and a little round belly
That shook, when he laughed, like a bowl full of jelly.
He was chubby and plump, a right jolly old elf,
And I laughed when I saw him, in spite of myself;
A wink of his eye and a twist of his head
Soon gave me to know I had nothing to dread;
He spoke not a word, but went straight to his work,
And filled all the stockings; then turned with a jerk,
And laying his finger aside of his nose,
And giving a nod, up the chimney he rose;
He sprang to his sleigh, to his team gave a whistle,
And away they all flew like the down of a thistle.
But I heard him exclaim, ere he drove out of sight,
'Happy Christmas to all, and to all a good night!'

Clement Clarke Moore

110

Christmas Is Coming

Christmas is coming,
The goose is getting fat,
Please to put a penny
In the old man's hat.
If you haven't got a penny
A ha'penny will do.
If you haven't got a ha'penny,
God bless you!

Anon.

Christmas Daybreak

Before the paling of the stars,
Before the winter morn,
Before the earliest cockcrow,
Jesus Christ was born:
Born in a stable,
Cradled in a manger,
In the world His hands had made,
Born a stranger.

Priest and king lay fast asleep
In Jerusalem,
Young and old lay fast asleep
in crowded Bethlehem:
Saint and angel, ox and ass,
Kept a watch together,
Before the Christmas daybreak
In the winter weather.

Jesus on His Mother's breast
In the stable cold,
Spotless Lamb of God was He,
Shepherd of the fold.
Let us kneel with Mary Maid,
With Joseph bent and hoary,
With saint and angel, ox and ass,
To hail the King of Glory.

Christina Rossetti

The Sea

The Tide Rises, the Tide Falls

The tide rises, the tide falls,
The twilight darkens, the curlew calls;
Along the sea-sands damp and brown
The traveller hastens toward the town;
   And the tide rises, the tide falls.

Darkness settles on roofs and walls,
But the sea in the darkness calls and calls;
The little waves, with their soft white hands,
Efface the footprints in the sands,
   And the tide rises, the tide falls.

The morning breaks; the steeds in their stalls
Stamp and neigh, as the hostler calls;
The day returns; but nevermore
Returns the traveller to the shore,
   And the tide rises, the tide falls.

Henry Wadsworth Longfellow

The Sea

The sea is a hungry dog,
Giant and grey.
He rolls on the beach all day.
With his clashing teeth and shaggy jaws
Hour upon hour he gnaws
The rumbling, tumbling stones,
And 'Bones, bones, bones!'
The giant sea-dog moans,
Licking his greasy paws.

And when the night wind roars
And the moon rocks in the stormy cloud,
He bounds to his feet and snuffs and sniffs,
Shaking his wet sides over the cliffs,
And howls and hollos long and loud.

But on quiet days in May or June,
When even the grasses on the dune
Play no more their reedy tune,
With his head between his paws
He lies on the sandy shores,
So quiet, so quiet, he scarcely snores.

James Reeves

Donkey Riding

Were you ever in Quebec,
Stowing timbers on a deck,
Where there's a king in his golden crown
 Riding on a donkey?

Hey ho, and away we go,
 Donkey riding, donkey riding,
Hey ho, and away we go,
 Riding on a donkey.

Were you ever in Cardiff Bay,
Where the folks all shout, Hooray!
Here comes John with his three months' pay,
 Riding on a donkey?

Hey ho, and away we go,
 Donkey riding, donkey riding,
Hey ho, and away we go,
 Riding on a donkey.

Were you ever off Cape Horn,
Where it's always fine and warm?
See the lion and the unicorn
 Riding on a donkey.

Hey ho, and away we go,
    Donkey riding, donkey riding,
Hey ho, and away we go,
    Riding on a donkey.

Anon.
English Sea Shanty

At the Seaside

When I was down beside the sea
A wooden spade they gave to me
    To dig the sandy shore.

My holes were empty like a cup.
In every hole the sea came up
    Till it could come no more.

Robert Louis Stevenson

The Horses of the Sea

The horses of the sea
Rear a foaming crest,
But the horses of the land
Serve us the best.
The horses of the land
Munch corn and clover,
While the foaming sea-horses
Toss and turn over.

Christina Rossetti

The Shell

And then I pressed the shell
   Close to my ear
And listened well,
And straightway like a bell
   Came low and clear
The slow, sad murmur of far distant seas,
Whipped by an icy breeze
   Upon a shore
Wind-swept and desolate.
   It was a sunless strand that never bore
The footprint of a man,
   Nor felt the weight

Since time began
Of any human quality or stir
Save what the dreary winds and waves incur.
And in the hush of waters was the sound
Of pebbles rolling round,
For ever rolling with a hollow sound.
And bubbling sea-weeds as the waters go
Swish to and fro
Their long, cold tentacles of slimy grey.
There was no day,
Nor ever came a night
Setting the stars alight
To wonder at the moon:
Was twilight only and the frightened croon,
Smitten to whimpers, of the dreary wind
And waves that journeyed blind –
And then I loosed my ear – oh, it was sweet
To hear a cart go jolting down the street!

James Stephens

Coral

'O sailor, come ashore,
   What have you brought for me?'
'Red coral, white coral,
   Coral from the sea.'

'I did not dig it from the ground,
    Nor pluck it from the tree;
Feeble insects made it
    In the stormy sea.'

Christina Rossetti

from *The Forsaken Merman*

Children dear, was it yesterday
(Call yet once) that she went away?
Once she sat with you and me,
On a red-gold throne in the heart of the sea,
And the youngest sat on her knee.
She combed its bright hair, and she tended it well,
When down swung the sound of the far-off bell.
She sighed, she looked up through the clear green sea,
She said, 'I must go, for my kinsfolk pray
In the little gray church on the shore today.
'Twill be Easter time in the world – ah me!
And I lose my poor soul, Merman, here with thee.'
I said, 'Go up, dear heart, through the waves:
Say thy prayer, and come back to the kind sea caves.'
She smiled, she went up through the surf in the bay,
    Children dear, was it yesterday?

Children dear, were we long alone?
'The sea grows stormy, the little ones moan;
Long prayers,' I said, 'in the world they say.'
'Come,' I said, and we rose through the surf in the bay.
We went up the beach, by the sandy down
Where the sea stocks bloom, to the white-walled town,
Through the narrow paved streets, where all was still,
To the little gray church on the windy hill.
From the church came a murmur of folk at their prayers,
But we stood without in the cold blowing airs.
We climbed on the graves, on the stones worn with rains,
And we gazed up the aisle through the small leaded panes.
She sat by the pillar; we saw her clear:
'Margaret, hist! come quick, we are here.
Dear heart,' I said, 'we are alone.
The sea grows stormy, the little ones moan.'
But, ah, she gave me never a look,
For her eyes were sealed to the holy book.
Loud prays the priest; shut stands the door.
Come away, children, call no more,
Come away, come down, call no more.

Down, down, down,
Down to the depths of the sea.
She sits at her wheel in the humming town,
Singing most joyfully.
Hark what she sings: 'O joy, O joy,
For the humming street, and the child with its toy!
For the priest, and the bell, and the holy well,
For the wheel where I spun

And the blessed light of the sun!'
And so she sings her fill,
Singing most joyfully,
Till the shuttle falls from her hand,
And the whizzing wheel stands still.
She steals to the window, and looks at the sand,
And over the sand at the sea;
And her eyes are set in a stare;
And anon there breaks a sign,
And anon there drops a tear,
From a sorrow-clouded eye,
And a heart sorrow-laden,
    A long, long sigh,
For the cold strange eyes of a little Mermaiden
And the gleam of her golden hair.

Matthew Arnold

from *The Mermaid*

Who would be
A mermaid fair,
Singing alone,
Combing her hair
Under the sea,
In a golden curl
With a comb of pearl,
on a throne?

Alfred, Lord Tennyson

from *The Merman*

Who would be
A merman bold,
Sitting alone
Singing alone
Under the sea,
With a crown of gold,
On a throne.

Alfred, Lord Tennyson

One Foot on Sea, and One on Shore

'Oh tell me once and tell me twice
    And tell me thrice to make it plain,
When we who part this weary day,
    When we who part shall meet again.'

'When windflowers blossom on the sea
    And fishes skim along the plain,
Then we who part this weary day,
    Then you and I shall meet again.'

'Yet tell me once before we part,
    Why need we part who part in pain?
If flowers must blossom on the sea,
    Why, we shall never meet again.

'My cheeks are paler than a rose,
   My tears are salter than the main,
My heart is like a lump of ice
   If we must never meet again.'

'Oh weep or laugh, but let me be,
   And live or die, for all's in vain;
For life's in vain since we must part,
   And parting must not meet again

'Till windflowers blossom on the sea
   And fishes skim along the plain;
Pale rose of roses, let me be, –
   Your breaking heart breaks mine again.'

Christina Rossetti

The Sands of Dee

'O Mary, go and call the cattle home,
   And call the cattle home,
   And call the cattle home
  Across the sands of Dee;'
The western wind was wild and dank with foam.
  And all alone went she.

The western tide crept up along the sand,
    And o'er and o'er the sand,
    And round and round the sand,
  As far as eye could see.
The rolling mist came down and hid the land:
  And never home came she.

'Oh! is it weed, or fish, or floating hair –
    A tress of golden hair,
    A drowned maiden's hair
  Above the nets at sea?
Was never salmon yet that shone so fair
  Among the stakes on Dee.'

They rowed her in across the rolling foam,
    The cruel crawling foam,
    The cruel hungry foam,
  To her grave beside the sea:
But still the boatmen hear her call the cattle home
  Across the sands of Dee.

Charles Kingsley

from *The Rime of the Ancient Mariner*

  'And now the Storm-blast came, and he
  Was tyrannous and strong:
  He struck with his o'ertaking wings,
  And chased us south along.

'With sloping masts and dipping prow,
As who pursued with yell and blow
Still treads the shadow of his foe,
And forward bends his head,
The ship drove fast, loud roar'd the blast,
And southward aye we fled.

'And now there came both mist and snow,
And it grew wondrous cold:
And ice, mast-high, came floating by,
As green as emerald.

'And through the drifts the snowy clifts
Did send a dismal sheen:
Nor shapes of men nor beasts we ken –
The ice was all between.

'The ice was here, the ice was there,
The ice was all around:
It crack'd and growl'd, and roar'd and howl'd,
Like noises in a swound!

'At length did cross an Albatross,
Thorough the fog it came;
As if it had been a Christian soul,
We hail'd it in God's name.

'It ate the food it ne'er had eat,
And round and round it flew.
The ice did split with a thunder-fit;
The helmsman steer'd us through!

'And a good south wind sprung up behind;
The Albatross did follow,
And every day, for food or play,
Came to the mariners' hollo!

'In mist or cloud, on mast or shroud,
It perch'd for vespers nine;
Whiles all the night, through fog-smoke white,
Glimmer'd the white moonshine.

'God save thee, ancient Mariner,
From the fiends, that plague thee thus! –
Why look'st thou so?' – 'With my crossbow
I shot the Albatross.

'The Sun now rose upon the right:
Out of the sea came he,
Still hid in mist, and on the left
Went down into the sea.

'And the good south wind still blew behind,
But no sweet bird did follow,
Nor any day for food or play
Came to the mariners' hollo!

'And I had done a hellish thing,
And it would work 'em woe:
For all averr'd I had kill'd the bird
That made the breeze to blow.
Ah wretch! said they, the bird to slay,
That made the breeze to blow!

'Nor dim nor red, like God's own head,
The glorious Sun uprist:
Then all averr'd I had kill'd the bird
That brought the fog and mist.
'Twas right, said they, such birds to slay,
That bring the fog and mist.

'The fair breeze blew, the white foam flew,
The furrow follow'd free;
We were the first that ever burst
Into that silent sea.

'Down dropt the breeze, the sails dropt down,
'Twas sad as sad could be;
And we did speak only to break
The silence of the sea!

'All in a hot and copper sky,
The bloody Sun, at noon,
Right up above the mast did stand,
No bigger than the Moon.

'Day after day, day after day,
We stuck, nor breath nor motion;
As idle as a painted ship
Upon a painted ocean.

'Water, water, everywhere,
    And all the boards did shrink;
Water, water, everywhere
    Nor any drop to drink.'

Samuel Taylor Coleridge

The Sailor's Consolation

One night came on a hurricane,
    The sea was mountains rolling,
When Barney Buntline turned his quid
    And said to Billy Bowling;
'A strong nor-wester's blowing, Bill:
    Hark, don't ye hear it roar, now?
Lord help 'em, how I pities them
    Unhappy folks on shore now!

'Foolhardy chaps who live in towns,
    What danger they are all in,
And now lie quaking in their beds,
    For fear the roof should fall in;
Poor creatures! how they envies us,
    And wishes, I've a notion,
For our good luck, in such a storm,
    To be upon the ocean!

'And as for them who're out all day
    On business from their houses,
And late at night are coming home,
    To cheer their babes and spouses,
While you and I, Bill, on the deck
    Are comfortably lying,
My eyes! what tiles and chimney-pots
    About their heads are flying!

'And very often have we heard
    How men are killed and undone
By overturns of carriages,
    By thieves, and fires in London;
We know what risks all landsmen run,
    From noblemen to tailors:
Then, Bill, let us thank Providence
    That you and I are sailors.'

                              Charles Dibdin

The Wreck of the Hesperus

It was the schooner Hesperus,
    That sailed the wintry sea;
And the skipper had taken his little daughter,
    To bear him company.

Blue were her eyes as the fairy-flax,
   Her cheeks like the dawn of day,
And her bosom white as the hawthorn buds
   That ope in the month of May.

The skipper he stood beside the helm,
   His pipe was in his mouth,
And he watched how the veering flaw did blow
   The smoke now West, now South.

Then up and spake an old Sailor,
   Had sailed the Spanish Main,
'I pray thee, put into yonder port,
   For I fear a hurricane.

'Last night the moon had a golden ring,
   And tonight no moon we see!'
The skipper he blew a whiff from his pipe,
   And a scornful laugh laughed he.

Colder and colder blew the wind,
   A gale from the North-east;
The snow fell hissing in the brine,
   And the billows frothed like yeast.

Down came the storm, and smote amain,
   The vessel in its strength;
She shuddered and paused, like a frightened steed,
   Then leaped her cable's length.

'Come hither! come hither! my little daughter,
    And do not tremble so;
For I can weather the roughest gale,
    That ever wind did blow.'

He wrapped her warm in his seaman's coat
    Against the stinging blast;
He cut a rope from a broken spar,
    And bound her to the mast.

'O father! I hear the churchbells ring,
    O say, what may it be?'
''Tis a fog-bell on a rock-bound coast!' –
    And he steered for the open sea.

'O father! I hear the sound of guns,
    O say, what may it be?'
'Some ship in distress, that cannot live
    In such an angry sea!'

'O father! I see a gleaming light,
    O say, what may it be?'
But the father answered never a word,
    A frozen corpse was he.

Lashed to the helm, all stiff and stark,
    With his face turned to the skies,
The lantern gleamed through the gleaming snow
    On his fixed and glassy eyes.

Then the maiden clasped her hands and prayed
    That savèd she might be;
And she thought of Christ, who stilled the wave,
    On the Lake of Galilee.

And fast through the midnight dark and drear,
    Through the whistling sleet and snow,
Like a sheeted ghost, the vessel swept
    Towards the reef of Norman's Woe.

And ever the fitful gusts between
    A sound came from the land;
It was the sound of the trampling surf,
    On the rocks and the hard sea-sand.

The breakers were right beneath her bows,
    She drifted a dreary wreck,
And a whooping billow swept the crew
    Like icicles from her deck.

She struck where the white and fleecy waves
    Looked soft as carded wool,
But the cruel rocks, they gored her side
    Like the horns of an angry bull.

Her rattling shrouds, all sheathed in ice,
    With the masts went by the board;
Like a vessel of glass, she stove and sank,
    Ho! Ho! the breakers roared!

At daybreak, on the bleak sea-beach,
  A fisherman stood aghast,
To see the form of a maiden fair,
  Lashed close to a drifting mast.

The salt sea was frozen on her breast,
  The salt tears in her eyes;
And he saw her hair, like the brown sea-weed,
  On the billows fall and rise.

Such was the wreck of the Hesperus,
  In the midnight and the snow!
Christ save us all from a death like this
  On the reef of Norman's Woe!

Henry Wadsworth Longfellow

Sea-Fever

I must down to the seas again, to the lonely sea and the
  sky,
And all I ask is a tall ship and a star to steer her by,
And a wheel's kick and the wind's song and the white sail's
  shaking,
And a grey mist on the sea's face and a grey dawn
  breaking.

I must down to the seas again, for the call of the running
  tide
Is a wild call and a clear call that may not be denied;
And all I ask is a windy day with the white clouds flying,
And the flung spray and the blown spume, and the seagulls
  crying.

I must down to the seas again, to the vagrant gypsy life,
To the gull's way and the whale's way where the wind's
  like a whetted knife;
And all I ask is a merry yarn from a laughing fellow-rover,
And quiet sleep and a sweet dream when the long trick's
  over.

John Masefield

The Inchcape Rock

No stir in the air, no stir in the sea –
The ship was as still as she could be;
Her sails from heaven received no motion;
Her keel was steady in the ocean.

Without either sign or sound of their shock,
The waves flowed over the Inchcape rock;
So little they rose, so little they fell,
They did not move the Inchcape bell.

The holy Abbot of Aberbrothok
Had placed that bell on the Inchcape rock;
On a buoy in the storm it floated and swung
And over the waves it warning rung.

When the rock was hid by the surges' swell,
The mariners heard the warning bell;
And then they knew the perilous rock,
And blessed the Abbot of Aberbrothok.

The sun in heaven was shining gay –
All things were joyful on that day;
The sea-birds screamed as they wheeled around,
And there was joyance in their sound.

The buoy of the Inchcape bell was seen,
A darker speck on the ocean green;
Sir Ralph, the rover, walked his deck,
And he fixed his eyes on the darker speck.

His eye was on the bell and float:
Quoth he, 'My men, put out the boat;
And row me to the Inchcape rock,
And I'll plague the priest of Aberbrothok.'

The boat is lowered, the boatmen row,
And to the Inchcape rock they go;
Sir Ralph bent over from the boat,
And cut the warning bell from the float.

Down sank the bell with a gurgling sound;
The bubbles rose, and burst around.
Quoth Sir Ralph, 'The next who comes to the rock
Will not bless the Abbot of Aberbrothok.'

Sir Ralph, the rover, sailed away –
He scoured the seas for many a day;
And now, grown rich with plundered store,
He steers his course to Scotland's shore.

So thick a haze o'erspreads the sky
They cannot see the sun on high;
The wind hath blown a gale all day;
At evening it hath died away.

On the deck the rover takes his stand;
So dark it is they see no land.
Quoth Sir Ralph, 'It will be lighter soon,
For there is the dawn of the rising moon.'

'Canst hear,' said one, 'the breakers roar?
For yonder, methinks, should be the shore.
Now where we are I cannot tell,
But I wish we could hear the Inchcape bell.'

They hear no sound; the swell is strong;
Though the wind hath fallen, they drift along;
Till the vessel strikes with a shivering shock –
O Christ! it is the Inchcape rock!

Sir Ralph, the rover, tore his hair;
He cursed himself in his despair.
The waves rush in on every side;
The ship is sinking beneath the tide.

But ever in his dying fear
One dreadful sound he seemed to hear –
A sound as if with the Inchcape bell
The Devil below was ringing his knell.

Robert Southey

The World Below the Brine

The world below the brine,
Forests at the bottom of the sea, the branches and leaves,
Sea-lettuce, vast lichens, strange flowers and seeds, the
    thick tangle, openings, and pink turf,
Different colours, pale grey and green, purple, white, and
    gold, the play of light through the water,
Dumb swimmers there among the rocks, coral, gluten,
    grass, rushes, and the aliment of the swimmers,
Sluggish existences grazing there suspended, or slowly
    crawling close to the bottom,
The sperm-whale at the surface blowing air and spray, or
    disporting with his flukes,
The leaden-eyed shark, the walrus, the turtle, the hairy sea-
    leopard, and the sting-ray,

Passions there, wars, pursuits, tribes, sight in those ocean-
depths, breathing that thick-breathing air, as so many
do,
The change thence to the sight here, and to the subtle air
breathed by beings like us who walk this sphere,
The change onward from ours to that of beings who walk
other spheres.

Walt Whitman

Song of the Galley-Slaves

We pulled for you when the wind was against us and the
sails were low.
    Will you never let us go?
We ate bread and onions when you took towns, or ran
aboard quickly when you were beaten by the foe.
The captains walked up and down the decks in fair
weather singing songs, but we were below.
We fainted with our chins on the oars and you did not see
that they were idle, for we still swung to and fro.
    Will you never let us go?
The salt made our oar-handles like shark-skin; our knees
were cut to the bone with salt-cracks; our hair was stuck
to our foreheads; and our lips were cut to the gums, and
you whipped us because we could not row.
    Will you never let us go?

But, in a little time, we shall run out of the port-holes as
the water runs along the oar-blade, and though you tell
the others to row after us you will never catch us till you
catch the oar-thresh and tie up the winds in the belly of
the sail. Aho!

Will you never let us go?

Rudyard Kipling

Thorkild's Song

There's no wind along these seas,
Out oars for Stavanger!
Forward all for Stavanger!
So we must wake the white-ash breeze,
Let fall for Stavanger!
A long pull for Stavanger!

Oh, hear the benches creak and strain!
(A long pull for Stavanger!)
She thinks she smells the Northland rain!
(A long pull for Stavanger!)

She thinks she smells the Northland snow,
And she's as glad as we to go.

She thinks she smells the Northland rime,
And the dear dark nights of winter-time.

She wants to be at her own home pier,
To shift her sails and standing gear.

She wants to be in her winter-shed,
To strip herself and go to bed.

Her very bolts are sick for shore,
And we – we want it ten times more!

So all you Gods that love brave men,
Send us a three-reef gale again!

Send us a gale, and watch us come,
With close-cropped canvas slashing home!

But – there's no wind on all these seas,
A long pull for Stavanger!
So we must wake the white-ash breeze.
A long pull for Stavanger!

Rudyard Kipling

from *Paradise Lost*
Book 7

Forthwith the sounds and seas, each creek and bay
With fry innumerable swarm, and shoals
Of fish that with their fins and shining scales
Glide under the green wave, in schools that oft
Bank the mid sea: part, single or with mate,
Graze the sea weed their pasture, and through groves
Of coral stray, or sporting with quick glance
Show to the sun their waved coats dropped with gold,
Or in their pearly shells at ease, attend
Moist nutriment, or under rocks their food
In jointed armour watch: on smooth the seal,
And bended dolphins play: part huge of bulk
Wallowing unwieldy, enormous in their gait
Tempest the ocean: there Leviathan
Hugest of living creatures, on the deep
Stretched like a promontory sleeps or swims,
And seems a moving land, and at his gills
Draws in, and at his trunk spouts out a sea.

John Milton

Dover Beach

The sea is calm tonight,
The tide is full, the moon lies fair
Upon the Straits; – on the French coast, the light
Gleams, and is gone; the cliffs of England stand,
Glimmering and vast, out in the tranquil bay.
Come to the window, sweet is the night air!
  Only, from the long line of spray
Where the ebb meets the moon-blanch'd land.
Listen! you hear the grating roar
Of pebbles which the waves suck back, and fling,
At their return, up the high strand,
Begin, and cease, and then again begin,
With tremulous cadence slow, and bring
The eternal note of sadness in.

  Sophocles long ago
Heard it on the Aegean, and it brought
Into his mind the turbid ebb and flow
  Of human misery; we
Find also in the sound a thought,
Hearing it by this distant northern sea.
  The sea of faith
Was once, too, at the full, and round earth's shore
Lay like the folds of a bright girdle furled;
  But now I only hear
Its melancholy, long, withdrawing roar,
  Retreating to the breath
Of the night-wind down the vast edges drear
And naked shingles of the world.

Ah, love, let us be true
To one another! for the world, which seems
To lie before us like a land of dreams,
So various, so beautiful, so new,
Hath really neither joy, nor love, nor light,
Nor certitude, nor peace, nor help for pain;
And we are here as on a darkling plain
Swept with confused alarms of struggle and flight,
Where ignorant armies clash by night.

Matthew Arnold

When Lamps Are Lighted in the Town

When lamps are lighted in the town
The boats sail out to sea.
The fishers watch when night comes down,
They watch for you and me.

You little children go to bed,
Before you sleep I pray
That God will watch the fishermen
And bring them home at day.

Anon.

Creatures

I think I could turn and live with animals

I think I could turn and live with animals, they are so
    placid and self-contained;
I stand and look at them long and long.
They do not sweat and whine about their condition;
They do not lie awake in the dark and weep for their sins;
They do not make me sick discussing their duty to God;
Not one is dissatisfied – not one is demented with the
    mania of owning things;
Not one kneels to another, nor to his kind that lived
    thousands of years ago;
Not one is respectable or industrious over the whole earth.

Walt Whitman

Be Like the Bird

Be like the bird, who
Resting in his flight
On a twig too slight
Feels it bend beneath him,
Yet sings
Knowing he has wings.

Victor Hugo

The Dog

The truth I do not stretch or shove
When I state the dog is full of love.
I've also proved, by actual test,
A wet dog is the lovingest.

Ogden Nash

Macavity: The Mystery Cat

Macavity's a Mystery Cat: he's called the Hidden Paw –
For he's the master criminal who can defy the Law.
He's the bafflement of Scotland Yard, the Flying Squad's despair:
For when they reach the scene of crime – *Macavity's not there!*

Macavity, Macavity, there's no one like Macavity,
He's broken every human law, he breaks the law of gravity.
His powers of levitation would make a fakir stare,
And when you reach the scene of crime – *Macavity's not there!*
You may seek him in the basement, you may look up in the air –
But I tell you once and once again, *Macavity's not there!*

Macavity's a ginger cat, he's very tall and thin;
You would know him if you saw him, for his eyes are
   sunken in.
His brow is deeply lined with thought, his head is highly
   domed;
His coat is dusty from neglect, his whiskers are uncombed.
He sways his head from side to side, with movements like
   a snake;
And when you think he's half asleep, he's always wide
   awake.

Macavity, Macavity, there's no one like Macavity,
For he's a fiend in feline shape, a monster of depravity.
You may meet him in a by-street, you may see him in the
   square –
But when a crime's discovered, then *Macavity's not there!*

He's outwardly respectable. (They say he cheats at cards.)
And his footprints are not found in any file of Scotland
   Yard's.
And when the larder's looted, or the jewel-case is rifled,
Or when the milk is missing, or another Peke's been stifled,
Or the greenhouse glass is broken, and the trellis past
   repair –
Ay, there's the wonder of the thing! *Macavity's not there!*

And when the Foreign Office find a Treaty's gone astray,
Or the Admiralty lose some plans and drawings by the
   way,
There may be a scrap of paper in the hall or on the stair –
But it's useless to investigate – *Macavity's not there!*
And when the loss has been disclosed, the Secret Service
   say:
'It *must* have been Macavity!' – but he's a mile away.
You'll be sure to find him resting, or a-licking of his
   thumbs,
Or engaged in doing complicated long division sums.

Macavity, Macavity, there's no one like Macavity,
There never was a Cat of such deceitfulness and suavity.
He always has an alibi, and one or two to spare:
At whatever time the deed took place – MACAVITY WASN'T
   THERE!
And they say that all the Cats whose wicked deeds are
   widely known,
(I might mention Mungojerrie, I might mention
   Griddlebone)
Are nothing more than agents for the Cat who all the time
Just controls their operations: the Napoleon of Crime.

                                                    T. S. Eliot

The Donkey

When fishes flew and forests walked
  And figs grew upon thorn,
Some moment when the moon was blood
  Then surely, I was born;

With monstrous head and sickening cry
  And ears like errant wings,
The devil's walking parody
  On all four-footed things.

The tattered outlaw of the earth,
  Of ancient crookèd will;
Starve, scourge, deride me: I am dumb,
  I keep my secret still.

Fools! For I also had my hour;
  One far fierce hour and sweet:
There was a shout about my ears,
  And palms before my feet.

G. K. Chesterton

The Vixen

Among the taller wood with ivy hung,
The old fox plays and dances round her young.
She snuffs and barks if any passes by
And swings her tail and turns prepared to fly.
The horseman hurries by, she bolts to see,
And turns agen, from danger never free.
If any stands she runs among the poles
And barks and snaps and drives them in the holes.
The shepherd sees them and the boy goes by
And gets a stick and progs the hole to try.
They get all still and lie in safety sure,
And out again when everything's secure,
And start and snap at blackbirds bouncing by
To fight and catch the great white butterfly.

John Clare

Mountain Lion

Climbing through the January snow into the Lobo canyon
Dark grow the spruce-trees, blue is the balsam, water
sounds still unfrozen, and the trail is still evident.

Men!
Two men!
Men! The only animal in the world to fear!

154

They hesitate.
We hesitate.
They have a gun.
We have no gun.

Then we all advance, to meet.

Two Mexicans, strangers, emerging out of the dark and
    snow and inwardness of the Lobo valley.
What are they doing here on this vanishing trail?

What is he carrying?
Something yellow.
A deer?

Qué tiene, amigo?
Leon –

He smiles, foolishly, as if he were caught doing wrong.
And we smile, foolishly, as if we didn't know.
He is quite gentle and dark-faced.

It is a mountain lion,
A long, long slim cat, yellow like a lioness.
Dead.

He trapped her this morning, he says, smiling foolishly.
Lift up her face,
Her round, bright face, bright as frost.
Her round, fine-fashioned head, with two dead ears;

And stripes in the brilliant frost of her face, sharp, fine
    dark rays,
Dark, keen, fine rays in the brilliant frost of her face.
Beautiful dead eyes.

Hermoso es!

They go out towards the open;
We go on into the gloom of Lobo.
And above the trees I found her lair,
A hole in the blood-orange brilliant rocks that stick up, a
    little cave.
And bones, and twigs, and a perilous ascent.

So, she will never leap up that way again, with the yellow
    flash of a mountain lion's long shoot!
And her bright striped frost-face will never watch any
    more, out of the shadow of the cave in the blood-orange
    rock,
Above the trees of the Lobo dark valley-mouth!

Instead, I look out.
And out to the dim of the desert, like a dream, never real;
To the snow of the Sangre de Cristo mountains, the ice of
    the mountains of Picoris,
And near across the opposite steep of snow, green trees
    motionless standing in snow, like a Christmas toy.

And I think in this empty world there was room for me
  and a mountain lion.
And I think in the world beyond, how easily we might
  spare a million or two of humans
And never miss them.
Yet what a gap in the world, the missing white frost-face
  of that slim yellow mountain lion!

D. H. Lawrence

The Dragon-Fly

Today I saw the dragon-fly
Come from the wells where he did lie.

An inner impulse rent the veil
Of his old husk: from head to tail
Came out clear plates of sapphire mail.
He dried his wings: like gauze they grew;
Thro' crofts and pastures wet with dew
A living flash of light he flew.

Alfred, Lord Tennyson

Hurt No Living Thing

Hurt no living thing;
Ladybird, nor butterfly,
Nor moth with dusty wing,
Nor cricket chirping cheerily,
Nor grasshopper so light of leap,
Nor dancing gnat, nor beetle fat,
Nor harmless worms that creep.

Christina Rossetti

Caterpillar

Brown and furry
Caterpillar in a hurry,
Take your walk
To the shady leaf, or stalk,
Or what not,
Which may be the chosen spot.
No toad spy you,
Hovering bird of prey pass by you;
Spin and die,
To live again a butterfly.

Christina Rossetti

The Snail

To grass, or leaf, or fruit, or wall
The snail sticks fast, nor fears to fall,
As if he grew there, house and all,
                   together.

Within that house secure he hides
When danger imminent betides,
Or storms, or other harms besides
               of weather.

Give but his horns the slightest touch,
His self-collecting power is such,
He shrinks into his house with much
                  displeasure.

Where'er he dwells, he dwells alone,
Except himself, has chattels none,
Well satisfied to be his own
                whole treasure.

Thus, hermit-like, his life he leads,
Nor partner of his banquet needs,
And if he meets one, only feeds
              the faster.

Who seeks him must be worse than blind,
(He and his house are so combined)
If finding it he fails to find

                    its master.

                    William Cowper

Ladybird! Ladybird!

Ladybird! Ladybird! Fly away home,
Night is approaching, and sunset is come:
The herons are flown to their trees by the Hall;
Felt, but unseen, the damp dewdrops fall.
This is the close of a still summer day;
Ladybird! Ladybird! haste! fly away!

                    Emily Brontë

Otters

I'll be an otter, and I'll let you swim
A mate beside me; we will venture down
A deep, full river when the sky above
Is shut of the sun; spoilers are we;
Thick-coated; no dog's tooth can bite at our veins –
With ears and eyes of poachers; deep-earthed ones

Turned hunters; let him slip past,
The little vole, my teeth are on an edge
For the King-fish of the River!

I hold him up –
The glittering salmon that smells of the sea;
I hold him up and whistle!

Now we go
Back to our earth; we will tear and eat
Sea-smelling salmon; you will tell the cubs
I am the Booty-bringer: I am the Lord
Of the River – the deep, dark, full, and flowing River!

Padraic Colum

How Doth the Little Crocodile

How doth the little crocodile
Improve his shining tail,
And pour the waters of the Nile
On every golden scale!

How cheerfully he seems to grin,
How neatly spreads his claws,
And welcomes little fishes in
With gently smiling jaws!

Lewis Carroll

The Rhinoceros

The rhino is a homely beast,
For human eyes he's not a feast,
But you and I will never know
Why nature chose to make him so.
Farewell, farewell, you old rhinoceros,
I'll stare at something less preposterous.

Ogden Nash

The Donkey

I saw a donkey
One day old,
His head was too big
For his neck to hold;
His legs were shaky
And long and loose,
They rocked and staggered
And weren't much use.

He tried to gambol
And frisk a bit,
But he wasn't quite sure
Of the trick of it.
His queer little coat
Was soft and grey,
And curled at his neck
In a lovely way.

He looked so little
And weak and slim,
I prayed the world
Might be good to him.

Anon.

The Fox

Mr Fox went out one chilly night,
And prayed to the moon to give him light,
For he'd many miles to go that night
Before he'd reach the town O!
  Town O! Town O!
For he'd many miles to go that night
Before he'd reach the town O!

He ran till he came to the farmer's yard,
Where the ducks and the geese declared it hard
That their nerves should be shaken and their rest so
  marred
By a visit from Mr Fox O!
  Fox O! Fox O!
That their nerves should be shaken and their rest so
  marred
By a visit from Mr Fox O!

He grabbed the grey goose by the neck,
And threw a duck across his back;
He didn't mind their quack, quack, quack,
And their legs all a-dangling down O!
  Down O! Down O!
He didn't mind their quack, quack, quack,
And their legs all a-dangling down O!

Old Mother Slipper Slopper jumped out of bed,
And out of the window she popped her head:
John, John, John, the grey goose is gone
And the fox is away to his den O!
  Den O! Den O!
John, John, John, the grey goose is gone
And the fox is away to his den O!

John ran up to the top of the hill,
And blew his horn both loud and shrill:
Fox said, I'd better flee with my kill,
Or they'll soon be on my trail O!
   Trail O! Trail O!
Fox said, I'd better flee with my kill,
Or they'll soon be on my trail O!

So he ran till he came to his cosy den,
And there were his little ones, eight, nine, ten:
They said, Daddy, better go back again
For it must be a mighty fine town O!
   Town O! Town O!
They said, Daddy, better go back again
For it must be a mighty fine town O!

Mr Fox and his wife, without any strife,
Cut up the goose with a carving knife:
They had never had such a meal in their life
And the little ones picked on the bones O!
   Bones O! Bones O!
They had never had such a meal in their life
And the little ones picked on the bones O!

Anon.

Lizard

A lizard ran out on a rock and looked up, listening
no doubt to the sounding of the spheres.
And what a dandy fellow! the right toss of a chin for you
and swirl of a tail!

If men were as much men as lizards are lizards
they'd be worth looking at.

D. H. Lawrence

The Flower-fed Buffaloes

The flower-fed buffaloes of the spring,
In the days of long ago,
Ranged where the locomotives sing
And the prairie flowers lie low: –
The tossing, blooming, perfumed grass
Is swept away by the wheat,
Wheels and wheels and wheels spin by
In the spring that still is sweet.
But the flower-fed buffaloes of the spring
Left us, long ago.
They gore no more, they bellow no more,
They trundle around the hills no more: –

With the Blackfeet, lying low,
With the Pawnees, lying low,
Lying low.

Vachel Lindsay

The Eagle

He clasps the crag with crooked hands;
Close to the sun in lonely lands,
Ring'd with the azure world, he stands.

The wrinkled sea beneath him crawls;
He watches from his mountain walls,
And like a thunderbolt he falls.

Alfred, Lord Tennyson

The Nightjar

We loved our Nightjar, but she would not stay with us.
We had found her lying as dead, but soft and warm,
Under the apple tree beside the old thatched wall.
Two days we kept her in a basket by the fire,
Fed her, and thought she well might live – till suddenly
In the very moment of most confiding hope

She raised herself all tense, quivered and drooped and died.
Tears sprang into my eyes – why not? the heart of man
Soon sets itself to love a living companion,
The more so if by chance it asks some care of him.
And this one had the kind of loveliness that goes
Far deeper than the optic nerve – full fathom five
To the soul's ocean cave, where Wonder and Reason
Tell their alternate dreams of how the world was made.
So wonderful she was – her wings the wings of night
But powdered here and there with tiny golden clouds
And wave-line markings like sea-ripples on the sand.
O how I wish I might never forget that bird –
Never!
     But even now, like all beauty of earth,
She is fading from me into the dusk of Time.

Sir Henry Newbolt

The Camel's Complaint

Canary-birds feed on sugar and seed,
    Parrots have crackers to crunch;
And as for the poodles, they tell me the noodles
    Have chicken and cream for their lunch.
      But there's never a question
      About *my* digestion –
        Anything does for me.

Cats, you're aware, can repose in a chair,
   Chickens can roost upon rails;
Puppies are able to sleep in a stable,
   And oysters can slumber in pails.
     But no one supposes
     A poor camel dozes –
       Any place does for me.

Lambs are enclosed where it's never exposed,
   Coops are constructed for hens;
Kittens are treated to houses well heated,
   And pigs are protected by pens.
     But a camel comes handy
     Wherever it's sandy –
       Anywhere does for me.

People would laugh if you rode a giraffe,
   Or mounted the back of an ox;
It's nobody's habit to ride on a rabbit,
   Or try to bestraddle a fox.
     But as for a camel, he's
     Ridden by families –
       Any load does for me.

A snake is as round as a hole in the ground,
   And weasels are wavy and sleek;
And no alligator could ever be straighter
   Than lizards that live in a creek.
     But a camel's all lumpy
     And bumpy and humpy –
       Any shape does for me.

Charles F. Carryl

The Tyger

Tyger! Tyger! burning bright
In the forests of the night,
What immortal hand or eye
Could frame thy fearful symmetry?

In what distant deeps or skies
Burnt the fire of thine eyes?
On what wings dare he aspire?
What the hand dare seize the fire?

And what shoulder, and what art,
Could twist the sinews of thy heart?
And, when thy heart began to beat,
What dread hand? and what dread feet?

What the hammer? what the chain?
In what furnace was thy brain?
What the anvil? what dread grasp
Dare its deadly terrors clasp?

When the stars threw down their spears,
And watered Heaven with their tears,
Did He smile His work to see?
Did He who made the Lamb make thee?

Tyger! Tyger! burning bright
In the forests of the night,
What immortal hand or eye
Dare frame thy fearful symmetry?

William Blake

The Gifts of the Animals to Man

The lion heart, the ounce gave active might,
The horse good shape, the sparrow lust to play,
Nightingale voice, enticing songs to say;
Elephant gave a perfect memory,
And parrot ready tongue, that to apply.

The fox gave craft, the dog gave flattery,
Ass patience, the mole a working thought,
Eagle high look, wolf secret cruelty,
Monkey sweet breath, the cow her fair eyes brought,
The ermine whitest skin, spotted with naught;
The sheep mild-seeming face, climbing the bear,
The stag did give the harm-eschewing fear.

The hare her sleights, the cat his melancholy,
Ant industry, and cony skill to build;
Cranes order, storks to be appearing holy;
Chameleon ease to change, duck ease to yield;
Crocodile, tears which might be falsely spill'd;
Ape great thing gave, though he did mowing stand,
The instrument of instruments, the hand.

Sir Philip Sidney

Choosing Their Names

Our old cat has kittens three –
What do you think their names should be?

One is a tabby with emerald eyes,
And a tail that's long and slender,
And into a temper she quickly flies
If you ever by chance offend her.
I think we shall call her this –
I think we shall call her that –
Now, don't you think that Pepperpot
Is a nice name for a cat?

One is black with a frill of white,
And her feet are all white fur,
If you stroke her she carries her tail upright
And quickly begins to purr.
I think we shall call her this –
I think we shall call her that –
Now, don't you think that Sootikin
Is a nice name for a cat?

One is a tortoiseshell yellow and black,
With plenty of white about him;
If you tease him, at once he sets up his back,
He's a quarrelsome one, ne'er doubt him.
I think we shall call him this –
I think we shall call him that –
Now don't you think that Scratchaway
Is a nice name for a cat?

Our old cat has kittens three
And I fancy these their names will be:
Pepperpot, Sootikin, Scratchaway – there!
Were ever kittens with these to compare?
And we call the old mother –
Now, what do you think? –
Tabitha Longclaws Tiddley Wink.

Thomas Hood

People

I *am Taliesin. I sing perfect metre*

I am Taliesin. I sing perfect metre,
Which will last to the end of the world.
My patron is Elphin . . .

I know why there is an echo in a hollow;
Why silver gleams; why breath is black; why liver is
    bloody;
Why a cow has horns; why a woman is affectionate;
Why milk is white; why holly is green;
Why a kid is bearded; why the cow-parsnip is hollow;
Why brine is salt; why ale is bitter;
Why the linnet is green and berries red;
Why a cuckoo complains; why it sings;
I know where the cuckoos of summer are in winter.
I know what beasts there are at the bottom of the sea;
How many spears in battle; how many drops in a shower;
Why a river drowned Pharaoh's people;
Why fishes have scales,
Why a white swan has black feet . . .

I have been a blue salmon,
I have been a dog, a stag, a roebuck on the mountain,
A stock, a spade, an axe in the hand,
A stallion, a bull, a buck,
A grain which grew on a hill,
I was reaped, and placed in an oven,
I fell to the ground when I was being roasted
And a hen swallowed me.
For nine nights was I in her crop.
I have been dead, I have been alive.
I am Taliesin.

Anon.

Brennan on the Moor

It's of a fearless highwayman a story I will tell,
His name was Willie Brennan and in Ireland he did dwell.
'Twas on the Kilworth mountains he began a wild career,
And many a noble gentleman before him shook with fear.

Crying Brennan's on the moor! Brennan's on the moor!
So bold and undaunted stood Bill Brennan on the moor.

'Twas on the King's own highway now Brennan he sat
   down,
He met the Mayor of Cashel just five miles out of town.
The Mayor he looked at Brennan and, 'I think now, boy,'
   says he,
'Your name is Billie Brennan; you must come along with
   me.'

Now Brennan's wife was going down town provisions for
   to buy,
And she seen Willie taken, ah sure she began to cry,
'Hand me ten pennies!' and sure just as he spoke,
She handed him a blunderbuss from underneath her cloak.

Brennan had his blunderbuss, my story I'll unfold,
He caused the Mayor of Cashel to deliver up his gold.
Five thousand pounds were offered for his apprehension
   there,
But Brennan and the pedlar to the mountain did repair.

Now Brennan is an outlaw upon a mountain high,
With Infantry and Cavalry to catch him they did try,
He laughed at them, he scorned at them until, it is said,
A false-hearted woman caused him to lose his head.

They hung him at the crossroads, in chains he swung and
   dried,
Some say in the midnight hour you still can see him ride.
You'll see him with his blunderbuss, and in the midnight
   chill
Along the King's own highway rides Willie Brennan still.

Anon.

The Highwayman

Part One

The wind was a torrent of darkness among the gusty
   trees,
The moon was a ghostly galleon tossed upon cloudy seas,
The road was a ribbon of moonlight over the purple moor,
And the highwayman came riding –
      Riding – riding –
The highwayman came riding, up to the old inn-door.

He'd a French cocked-hat on his forehead, a bunch of lace
   at his chin,
A coat of the claret velvet, and breeches of brown doeskin:
They fitted with never a wrinkle; his boots were up to the
   thigh!
And he rode with a jewelled twinkle,
      His pistol butts a-twinkle,
His rapier hilt a-twinkle, under the jewelled sky.

Over the cobbles he clattered and clashed in the dark inn-
    yard,
And he tapped with his whip on the shutters, but all was
    locked and barred:
He whistled a tune to the window, and who should be
    waiting there
But the landlord's black-eyed daughter,
      Bess, the landlord's daughter,
Plaiting a dark red love-knot into her long black hair.

And dark in the dark old inn-yard a stable-wicket creaked
Where Tim, the ostler, listened; his face was white and
    peaked,
His eyes were hollows of madness, his hair like mouldy
    hay;
But he loved the landlord's daughter,
      The landlord's red-lipped daughter:
Dumb as a dog he listened, and he heard the robber say –

'One kiss, my bonny sweetheart, I'm after a prize tonight,
But I shall be back with the yellow gold before the
    morning light.
Yet if they press me sharply, and harry me through the day,
Then look for me by moonlight:
      Watch for me by moonlight:
I'll come to thee by moonlight, though Hell should bar the
    way.'

He rose upright in the stirrups, he scarce could reach her
   hand;
But she loosened her hair i' the casement! His face burnt
   like a brand
As the black cascade of perfume came tumbling over his
   breast;
And he kissed its waves in the moonlight,
     (Oh, sweet black waves in the moonlight)
Then he tugged at his reins in the moonlight, and galloped
   away to the West.

Part Two

He did not come in the dawning; he did not come at noon;
And out of the tawny sunset, before the rise o' the moon,
When the road was a gypsy's ribbon, looping the purple
   moor,
A red-coat troop came marching –
     Marching – marching –
King George's men came marching, up to the old inn-door.

They said no word to the landlord, they drank his ale
   instead;
But they gagged his daughter and bound her to the foot of
   her narrow bed.
Two of them knelt at her casement, with muskets at the
   side!
There was death at every window;
     And Hell at one dark window;
For Bess could see, through her casement, the road that *he*
   would ride.

They had tied her up to attention, with many a sniggering
    jest:
They had bound a musket beside her, with the barrel
    beneath her breast!
'Now keep good watch!' and they kissed her.
       She heard the dead man say –
Look for me by moonlight;
     Watch for me by moonlight;
I'll come to thee by moonlight, though Hell should bar the
    way!

She twisted her hands behind her; but all the knots held
    good!
She writhed her hands till her fingers were wet with sweat
    or blood!
They stretched and strained in the darkness, and the hours
    crawled by like years;
Till, now, on the stroke of midnight,
     Cold, on the stroke of midnight,
The tip of one finger touched it! The trigger at least was
    hers!

The tip of one finger touched it; she strove no more for the
    rest!
Up, she stood up to attention, with the barrel beneath her
    breast,
She would not risk their hearing; she would not strive again;
For the road lay bare in the moonlight,
     Blank and bare in the moonlight;
And the blood of her veins in the moonlight throbbed to
    her Love's refrain.

Tlot-tlot, tlot-tlot! Had they heard it? The horse-hoofs
  ringing clear –
Tlot-tlot, tlot-tlot, in the distance? Were they deaf that they
  did not hear?
Down the ribbon of moonlight, over the brow of the hill,
The highwayman came riding,
    Riding, riding!
The red-coats looked to their priming! She stood up
  straight and still!

Tlot-tlot, in the frosty silence! *Tlot-tlot* in the echoing
  night!
Nearer he came and nearer! Her face was like a light!
Her eyes grew wide for a moment; she drew one last deep
  breath,
Then her finger moved in the moonlight,
    Her musket shattered the moonlight,
Shattered her breast in the moonlight and warned him –
  with her death.

He turned; he spurred him westward; he did not know
  who stood
Bowed with her head o'er the musket, dreached with her
  own red blood!
Not till the dawn he heard it, and slowly blanched to hear
How Bess, the landlord's daughter,
    The landlord's black-eyed daughter,
Had watched for her Love in the moonlight; and died in
  the darkness there.

Back, he spurred like a madman, shrieking a curse to the
 sky,
With the white road smoking behind him, and his rapier
 brandished high!
Blood-red were his spurs i' the golden noon; wine-red was
 his velvet coat;
When they shot him down on the highway,
    Down like a dog on the highway,
And he lay in his blood on the highway, with the bunch of
 lace at his throat.

And still of a winter's night, they say, when the wind is in
 the trees,
When the moon is a ghostly galleon tossed upon cloudy
 seas,
When the road is a ribbon of moonlight over the purple
 moor,
A highwayman comes riding –
    Riding – riding –
A highwayman comes riding, up to the old inn-door.

Over the cobbles he clatters and clangs in the dark inn-yard;
And he taps with his whip on the shutters, but all is locked
 and barred:
He whistles a tune to the window, and who should be
 waiting there
But the landlord's black-eyed daughter,
    Bess, the landlord's daughter,
Plaiting a dark red love-knot into her long black hair.

Alfred Noyes

The Pied Piper of Hamelin

I

Hamelin Town's in Brunswick,
By famous Hanover city;
The river Weser, deep and wide,
Washes its wall on the southern side;
A pleasanter spot you never spied;
But, when begins my ditty,
Almost five hundred years ago,
To see the townsfolk suffer so
From vermin, was a pity.

II

Rats!
They fought the dogs and killed the cats,
And bit the babies in the cradles,
And ate the cheeses out of the vats,
And licked the soup from the cooks' own ladles,
Split open the kegs of salted sprats,
Made nests inside men's Sunday hats,
And even spoiled the women's chats
By drowning their speaking
With shrieking and squeaking
In fifty different sharps and flats.

III

At last the people in a body
To the town hall came flocking:
''Tis clear,' cried they, 'our Mayor's a noddy;
And as for our Corporation – shocking
To think we buy gowns lined with ermine
For dolts that can't or won't determine
What's best to rid us of our vermin!
You hope, because you're old and obese,
To find in the furry civic robe ease?
Rouse up, sirs! Give your brains a racking
To find the remedy we're lacking,
Or, sure as fate, we'll send you packing!'
At this the Mayor and Corporation
Quaked with a mighty consternation.

IV

An hour they sat in council,
At length the Mayor broke silence:
'For a guilder I'd my ermine gown sell,
I wish I were a mile hence!
It's easy to bid one rack one's brain –
I'm sure my poor head aches again,
I've scratched it so, and all in vain,
Oh for a trap, a trap, a trap!'
Just as he said this, what should hap
At the chamber door but a gentle tap?
'Bless us,' cried the Mayor, 'what's that?'
(With the Corporation as he sat,

Looking little though wondrous fat;
Nor brighter was his eye, nor moister
Than a too-long-opened oyster,
Save when at noon his paunch grew mutinous
For a plate of turtle, green and glutinous)
'Only a scraping of shoes on the mat?
Anything like the sound of a rat
Makes my heart go pit-a-pat!'

V

'Come in!' – the Mayor cried, looking bigger:
And in did come the strangest figure!
His queer long coat from heel to head
Was half of yellow and half of red
And he himself was tall and thin,
With sharp blue eyes, each like a pin,
And light loose hair, yet swarthy skin,
No tuft on cheek nor beard on chin,
But lips where smiles went out and in –
There was no guessing his kith and kin!
And nobody could enough admire
The tall man and his quaint attire.
Quoth one: 'It's as if my great-grandsire,
Starting up at the Trump of Doom's tone,
Had walked this way from his painted tombstone!'

VI

He advanced to the council-table:
And, 'Please your honours,' said he, 'I'm able,
By means of a secret charm, to draw
All creatures living beneath the sun,
That creep or swim or fly or run,
After me so as you never saw!
And I chiefly use my charm
On creatures that do people harm,
The mole and toad and newt and viper;
And people call me the Pied Piper.'
(And here they noticed round his neck
A scarf of red and yellow stripe,
To match with his coat of the self-same check;
And at the scarf's end hung a pipe;
And his fingers, they noticed, were ever straying
As if impatient to be playing
Upon this pipe, as low it dangled
Over his vesture so old-fangled.)
'Yet,' said he, 'poor piper as I am,
In Tartary I freed the Cham,
Last June, from his huge swarm of gnats;
I eased in Asia the Nizam
Of a monstrous brood of vampyre-bats:
And as for what your brain bewilders –
If I can rid your town of rats
Will you give me a thousand guilders?'
'One? Fifty thousand!' was the exclamation
Of the astonished Mayor and Corporation.

VII

Into the street the Piper stept,
Smiling first a little smile,
As if he knew what magic slept
In his quiet pipe the while;
Then, like a musical adept,
To blow the pipe his lips he wrinkled,
And green and blue his sharp eyes twinkled,
Like a candle-flame where salt is sprinkled;
And ere three shrill notes the pipe uttered,
You heard as if an army muttered;
And the muttering grew to a grumbling;
And the grumbling grew to a mighty rumbling;
And out of the houses the rats came tumbling.
Great rats, small rats, lean rats, brawny rats,
Brown rats, black rats, grey rats, tawny rats,
Grave old plodders, gay young friskers,
Fathers, mothers, uncles, cousins.
Cocking tails and pricking whiskers,
Families by tens and dozens,
Brothers, sisters, husbands, wives
Followed the Piper for their lives.
From street to street he piped advancing,
And step for step they followed dancing,
Until they came to the river Weser
Wherein all plunged and perished!
Save one who, stout as Julius Caesar,
Swam across and lived to carry
(As the manuscript he cherished)
To Rat-land home his commentary:

Which was, 'At the first shrill notes of the pipe,
I heard a sound as of scraping tripe,
And putting apples, wondrous ripe,
Into a cider-press's gripe:
And a moving away of pickle-tub-boards,
And a leaving ajar of conserve-cupboards,
And a drawing the corks of train-oil-flasks,
And a breaking the hoops of butter-casks:
And it seemed as if a voice
(Sweeter far than by harp or by psaltery
Is breathed) called out, "Oh rats, rejoice!
The world is grown to one vast dry-saltery!
So munch on, crunch on, take your nuncheon,
Breakfast, supper, dinner, luncheon!"
And just as a bulky sugar-puncheon,
All ready staved, like a great sun shone
Glorious scarce an inch before me,
Just as methought it said "Come bore me!"
– I found the Weser rolling o'er me.'

VIII

You should have heard the Hamelin people
Ringing the bells till they rocked the steeple.
'Go,' cried the Mayor, 'and get long poles!
Poke out the nests and block up the holes!
Consult with carpenters and builders
And leave in our town not even a trace
Of the rats!' – when suddenly, up the face
Of the Piper perked in the market-place,
With a, 'First, if you please, my thousand guilders!'

IX

A thousand guilders! The Mayor looked blue;
So did the Corporation too.
For council dinners made rare havoc
With Claret, Moselle, Vin-de-Grave, Hock;
And half the money would replenish
Their cellar's biggest butt with Rhenish.
To pay this sum to a wandering fellow
With a gypsy coat of red and yellow!
'Beside,' quoth the Mayor with a knowing wink,
'Our business was done at the river's brink;
We saw with our eyes the vermin sink.
And what's dead can't come to life, I think.
So, friend, we're not the folks to shrink
From the duty of giving you something for drink,
And a matter of money to put in your poke;
But as for the guilders, what we spoke
Of them, as you very well know, was in joke.
Beside, our losses have made us thrifty.
A thousand guilders! Come, take fifty!'

X

The Piper's face fell, and he cried,
'No trifling! I can't wait! Beside,
I've promised to visit by dinnertime
Bagdad, and accept the prime
Of the Head-Cook's pottage, all he's rich in,
For having left, in the Caliph's kitchen,
Of a nest of scorpions no survivor –
With him I proved no bargain-driver,

With you, don't think I'll bate a stiver!
And folks who put me in a passion
May find me pipe to another fashion.'

XI

'How?' cried the Mayor, 'd'ye think I brook
Being worse treated than a Cook?
Insulted by a lazy ribald
With idle pipe and vesture piebald?
You threaten us, fellow? Do your worst,
Blow your pipe there till you burst!'

XII

Once more he stept into the street
And to his lips again
Laid his long pipe of smooth straight cane;
And ere he blew three notes (such sweet
Soft notes as yet musician's cunning
Never gave the enraptured air)
There was a rustling that seemed like a bustling
Of merry crowds justling at pitching and hustling,
Small feet were pattering, wooden shoes clattering,
Little hands clapping, and little tongues chattering,
And, like fowls in a farm-yard when barley is scattering,
Out came the children running.
All the little boys and girls,
With rosy cheeks and flaxen curls,
And sparkling eyes and teeth like pearls,
Tripping and skipping, ran merrily after
The wonderful music with shouting and laughter.

XIII

The Mayor was dumb, and the Council stood
As if they were changed into blocks of wood,
Unable to move a step or cry,
To the children merrily skipping by –
And could only follow with the eye
That joyous crowd at the Piper's back.
But how the Mayor was on the rack
And the wretched Council's bosoms beat,
As the Piper turned from the High Street
To where the Weser rolled its waters
Right in the way of their sons and daughters!
However he turned from South to West
And to Koppelberg Hill his steps addressed,
And after him the children pressed;
Great was the joy in every breast.
'He never can cross that mighty top!
He's forced to let the piping drop
And we shall see our children stop!'
When, lo, as they reached the mountain-side,
A wondrous portal opened wide,
As if a cavern was suddenly hollowed;
And the Piper advanced and the children followed,
And when all were in to the very last,
The door in the mountain-side shut fast.
Did I say all? No! One was lame,
And could not dance the whole of the way;
And in after years, if you would blame
His sadness, he was used to say, –
'It's dull in our town since my playmates left!

194

I can't forget that I'm bereft
Of all the pleasant sights they see,
Which the Piper also promised me.
For he led us, he said, to a joyous land,
Joining the town and just at hand,
Where waters gushed and fruit-trees grew,
And flowers put forth a fairer hue,
And everything was strange and new;
The sparrows were brighter than peacocks here,
And their dogs outran our fallow deer,
And honey-bees had lost their stings,
And horses were born with eagles' wings:
And just as I became assured
My lame foot would be speedily cured,
The music stopped and I stood still,
And found myself outside the hill,
Left alone against my will,
To go now limping as before,
And never hear of that country more!'

XIV

Alas, alas for Hamelin!
There came into many a burgher's pate
A text which says that heaven's gate
Opens to the rich at as easy rate
As the needle's eye takes a camel in!
The mayor sent East, West, North and South,
To offer the Piper, by word of mouth
Wherever it was men's lot to find him,
Silver and gold to his heart's content,

If he'd only return the way he went,
And bring the children behind him.
But when they saw 'twas a lost endeavour,
And Piper and dancers were gone forever,
They made a decree that lawyers never
Should think their records dated duly
If, after the day of the month and year,
These words did not as well appear:
'And so long after what happened here
On the twenty-second of July,
Thirteen hundred and seventy-six;'
And the better in memory to fix
The place of the children's last retreat,
They called it the Pied Piper's Street,
Where any one playing on pipe or tabor
Was sure for the future to lose his labour.
Nor suffered they hostelry or tavern
To shock with mirth a street so solemn,
But opposite the place of the cavern
They wrote the story on a column,
And on the great church-window painted
The same, to make the world acquainted
How their children were stolen away,
And there it stands to this very day.
And I must not omit to say
That, in Transylvania there's a tribe
Of alien people who ascribe
To the outlandish ways and dress
On which their neighbours lay such stress,
To their fathers and mothers having risen

Out of some subterranean prison
Into which they were trepanned
Long time ago in a mighty band
Out of Hamelin town in Brunswick land,
But how or why they don't understand.

XV

So, Willy, let you and me be wipers
Of scores out with all men – especially pipers!
And, whether they pipe us free from rats or from mice,
If we've promised them aught, let us keep our promise.

Robert Browning

The Pirate

He walks the deck with swaggering gait,
(There's mischief in his eye)
Pedigree Pirate through and through,
With pistols, dirk and cutlass too;
A rollicking rip with scars to show
For every ship he's sent below.
His tongue is quick, his temper high,
And whenever he speaks they shout, 'Ay, Ay!'
To this king of a roaring crew.

His ship's as old as the sea herself,
And foggity foul is she:
But what cares he for foul or fine?
If guns don't glitter and decks don't shine?
For sailormen from East to West
Have walked the plank at his request;
But if he's caught you may depend
He'll dangle high at the business end
Of a tickly, tarry line.

Hugh Chesterman

Gypsies

The gypsies seek wide sheltering woods again,
With droves of horses flock to mark their lane,
And trample on dead leaves, and hear the sound,
And look and see the black clouds gather round,
And set their camps, and free from muck and mire,
And gather stolen sticks to make the fire.
The roasted hedgehog, bitter though as gall,
Is eaten up and relished by them all.
They know the woods and every fox's den
And get their living far away from men;
The shooters ask them where to find the game,
The rabbits know them and are almost tame.
The aged women, tawny with the smoke,
Go with the winds and crack the rotted oak.

John Clare

The Raggle Taggle Gypsies

'Twas late last night when my lord came home,
  Inquiring for his lady, O.
The servants said on every hand,
  'She's gone with the Raggle Taggle Gypsies, O.'

'Oh, saddle for me my milk-white steed,
  Oh, saddle for me my pony, O,
That I may ride and seek my bride
  Who's gone with the Raggle Taggle Gypsies, O.'

Oh, he rode high and he rode low,
  He rode through woods and copses, O,
Until he came to an open field,
  And there he espied his lady, O.

'What makes you leave your house and lands?
  What makes you leave your money, O?
What makes you leave your new-wedded lord
  To go with the Raggle Taggle Gypsies, O?'

'What care I for my house and lands?
  What care I for my money, O?
What care I for my new-wedded lord?
  I'm off with the Raggle Taggle Gypsies, O.'

'Last night you slept on a goose-feather bed,
 With the sheet turned down so bravely, O.
Tonight you will sleep in the cold, open field,
 Along with the Raggle Taggle Gypsies, O.'

'What care I for your goose-feather bed,
 With the sheet turned down so bravely, O?
For tonight I shall sleep in a cold, open field,
 Along with the Raggle Taggle Gypsies, O.'

Anon.

Meg Merrilees

Old Meg she was a Gypsy,
 And lived upon the moors:
Her bed it was the brown heath turf,
 And her house was out of doors.

Her apples were swart blackberries,
 Her currants pods o' broom;
Her wine was dew of the wild white rose,
 Her book a churchyard tomb.

Her Brothers were the craggy hills,
 Her Sisters larchen trees;
Alone with her great family
 She lived as she did please.

No breakfast had she many a morn,
  No dinner many a noon,
And 'stead of supper she would stare
  Full hard against the Moon.

But every morn of woodbine fresh
  She made her garlanding,
And every night the dark glen Yew
  She wove, and she would sing.

And with her fingers, old and brown,
  She plaited Mats o' Rushes,
And gave them to the Cottagers
  She met among the Bushes.

Old Meg was brave as Margaret Queen,
  And tall as Amazon;
An old red blanket cloak she wore;
  A chip hat had she on.
God rest her agèd bones somewhere –
  She died full long agone!

John Keats

A Smugglers' Song

If you wake at midnight and hear a horse's feet,
Don't go drawing back the blind, or looking down the
    street,
Them that asks no questions isn't told a lie.
Watch the wall, my darling, while the Gentlemen go by!
      Five and twenty ponies,
      Trotting through the dark –
      Brandy for the Parson,
      'Baccy for the Clerk;
      Laces for the lady; letters for a spy,
And watch the wall, my darling, while the Gentlemen go
    by!

Running round the woodlump if you chance to find
Little barrels, roped and tarred, all full of brandy-wine;
Don't you shout to come and look, nor take 'em for your
    play;
Put the brushwood back again – and they'll be gone next
    day!

If you see the stableyard setting open wide;
If you see a tired horse lying down inside;
If your mother mends a coat cut about and tore;
If the lining's wet and warm – don't you ask no more!

If you meet King George's men, dressed in blue and red,
You be careful what you say, and mindful what is said.
If they call you 'pretty maid', and chuck you 'neath the
chin,
Don't you tell where no one is, nor yet where no one's
been!

Knocks and footsteps round the house – whistles after
dark –
You've no call for running out till the housedogs bark.
Trusty's here and Pincher's here, and see how dumb they
lie –
They don't fret to follow when the Gentlemen go by!

If you do as you've been told, likely there's a chance,
You'll be give a dainty doll, all the way from France,
With a cap of Valenciennes, and a velvet hood –
A present from the Gentlemen, along o' being good!
        Five and twenty ponies,
        Trotting through the dark –
        Brandy for the Parson,
        'Baccy for the Clerk.
Them that asks no questions isn't told a lie –
Watch the wall, my darling, while the Gentlemen go by!

Rudyard Kipling

from *The Song Of Hiawatha*

Swift of foot was Hiawatha;
He could shoot an arrow from him,
And run forward with such fleetness,
That the arrow fell behind him!
Strong of arm was Hiawatha;
He could shoot ten arrows upward,
Shoot them with such strength and swiftness,
That the tenth had left the bow-string
Ere the first to earth had fallen!
  He had mittens, Minjekahwun,
Magic mittens made of deer-skin;
When upon his hands he wore them,
He could smite the rocks asunder,
He could grind them into powder.
He had moccasins enchanted,
Magic moccasins of deer-skin;
When he bound them round his ankles,
When upon his feet he tied them,
At each stride a mile he measured!

Henry Wadsworth Longfellow

The Lady of Shalott

Part I

On either side the river lie
Long fields of barley and of rye,
That clothe the wold and meet the sky;
And thro' the field the road runs by
      To many-tower'd Camelot;
And up and down the people go,
Gazing where the lilies blow
Round an island there below,
      The island of Shalott.

Willows whiten, aspens quiver,
Little breezes dusk and shiver
Thro' the wave that runs for ever
By the island in the river
      Flowing down to Camelot.
Four grey walls, and four grey towers,
Overlook a space of flowers,
And the silent isle imbowers
      The Lady of Shalott.

By the margin, willow-veil'd,
Slide the heavy barges trail'd
By slow horses; and unhail'd
The shallop flitteth silken-sail'd
     Skimming down to Camelot:
But who hath seen her wave her hand?
Or at the casement seen her stand?
Or is she known in all the land,
     The Lady of Shalott?

Only reapers, reaping early
In among the bearded barley,
Hear a song that echoes cheerly
From the river winding clearly,
     Down to tower'd Camelot:
And by the moon the reaper weary,
Piling sheaves in uplands airy,
Listening, whispers ''Tis the fairy
     Lady of Shalott.'

Part II

There she weaves by night and day
A magic web with colours gay.
She has heard a whisper say,
A curse is on her if she stay
     To look down to Camelot.
She knows not what the curse may be,
And so she weaveth steadily,
And little other care hath she,
     The Lady of Shalott.

And moving thro' a mirror clear
That hangs before her all the year,
Shadows of the world appear.
There she sees the highway near
      Winding down to Camelot:
There the river eddy whirls,
And there the surly village-churls,
And the red cloaks of market girls,
      Pass onward from Shalott.

Sometimes a troop of damsels glad,
An abbot on an ambling pad,
Sometimes a curly shepherd-lad,
Or long-hair'd page in crimson clad,
      Goes by to tower'd Camelot:
And sometimes thro' the mirror blue
The knights come riding two and two:
She hath no loyal knight and true,
      The Lady of Shalott.

But in her web she still delights
To weave the mirror's magic sights,
For often thro' the silent nights
A funeral, with plumes and lights,
      And music, went to Camelot:
Or when the moon was overhead,
Came two young lovers lately wed;
'I am half sick of shadows,' said
      The Lady of Shalott.

Part III

A bow-shot from her bower-eaves,
He rode between the barley-sheaves,
The sun came dazzling thro' the leaves,
And flamed upon the brazen greaves
    Of bold Sir Lancelot.
A red-cross knight for ever kneel'd
To a lady in his shield,
That sparkled on the yellow field,
    Beside remote Shalott.

The gemmy bridle glitter'd free,
Like to some branch of stars we see
Hung in the golden Galaxy.
The bridle bells rang merrily
    As he rode down to Camelot:
And from his blazon'd baldric slung
A mighty silver bugle hung,
And as he rode his armour rung,
    Beside remote Shalott.

All in the blue unclouded weather
Thick-jewell'd shone the saddle-leather,
The helmet and the helmet-feather
Burn'd like one burning flame together,
    As he rode down to Camelot.
As often thro' the purple night,
Below the starry clusters bright,
Some bearded meteor, trailing light,
    Moves over still Shalott.

His broad clear brow in sunlight glow'd;
On burnish'd hooves his war-horse trode;
From underneath his helmet flow'd
His coal-black curls as on he rode,
    As he rode down to Camelot.
From the bank and from the river
He flash'd into the crystal mirror,
'Tirra lira,' by the river
    Sang Sir Lancelot.

She left the web, she left the loom,
She made three paces thro' the room,
She saw the water-lily bloom,
She saw the helmet and the plume,
    She look'd down to Camelot.
Out flew the web and floated wide;
The mirror crack'd from side to side;
'The curse is come upon me,' cried
    The Lady of Shalott.

Part IV

In the stormy east-wind straining,
The pale yellow woods were waning,
The broad stream in his banks complaining,
Heavily the low sky raining
    Over tower'd Camelot;
Down she came and found a boat
Beneath a willow left afloat,
And round about the prow she wrote
    The Lady of Shalott.

And down the river's dim expanse –
Like some bold seer in a trance,
Seeing all his own mischance –
With a glassy countenance
      Did she look to Camelot.
And at the closing of the day
She loosed the chain, and down she lay;
The broad stream bore her far away,
      The Lady of Shalott.

Lying, robed in snowy white
That loosely flew to left and right –
The leaves upon her falling light –
Thro' the noises of the night
      She floated down to Camelot:
And as the boat-head wound along
The willowy hills and fields among,
They heard her singing her last song,
      The Lady of Shalott.

Heard a carol, mournful, holy,
Chanted loudly, chanted lowly,
Till her blood was frozen slowly,
And her eyes were darken'd wholly,
      Turn'd to tower'd Camelot.
For ere she reach'd upon the tide
The first house by the water-side,
Singing in her song she died,
      The Lady of Shalott.

Under tower and balcony,
By garden-wall and gallery,
A gleaming shape she floated by,
Dead-pale between the houses high,
    Silent into Camelot.
Out upon the wharfs they came,
Knight and burgher, lord and dame,
And round the prow they read her name,
    The Lady of Shalott.

Who is this? and what is here?
And in the lighted palace near
Died the sound of royal cheer;
And they cross'd themselves for fear,
    All the knights at Camelot:
But Lancelot mused a little space;
He said, 'She has a lovely face;
God in his mercy lend her grace,
    The Lady of Shalott.'

Alfred, Lord Tennyson

Matilda

Who told Lies, and was Burned to Death

Matilda told such Dreadful Lies,
It made one Gasp and Stretch one's Eyes;
Her Aunt, who, from her Earliest Youth,
Had kept a Strict Regard for Truth,
Attempted to Believe Matilda:
The effort very nearly killed her,
And would have done so, had not She
Discovered this Infirmity.
For once, towards the Close of Day,
Matilda, growing tired of play,
And finding she was left alone,
Went tiptoe to the Telephone
And summoned the Immediate Aid
Of London's Noble Fire-Brigade.
Within an hour the Gallant Band
Were pouring in on every hand,
From Putney, Hackney Downs and Bow,
With Courage high and Hearts a-glow
They galloped, roaring through the Town,
'Matilda's House is Burning Down!'
Inspired by British Cheers and Loud
Proceeding from the Frenzied Crowd,
They ran their ladders through a score
Of windows on the Ball Room Floor;
And took Peculiar Pains to Souse
The Pictures up and down the House,

Until Matilda's Aunt succeeded
In showing them they were not needed,
And even then she had to pay
To get the Men to go away!

It happened that a few Weeks later
Her Aunt was off to the Theatre
To see that Interesting Play
The Second Mrs Tanqueray.
She had refused to take her Niece
To hear this Entertaining Piece:
A Deprivation Just and Wise
To Punish her for Telling Lies.
That Night a Fire *did* break out –
You should have heard Matilda Shout!
You should have heard her Scream and Bawl,
And throw the window up and call
To People passing in the Street –
(The rapidly increasing Heat
Encouraging her to obtain
Their confidence) – but all in vain!
For every time she shouted 'Fire!'
They only answered 'Little Liar!'
And therefore when her Aunt returned,
Matilda, and the House, were Burned.

Hilaire Belloc

People

I like people quite well
at a little distance.
I like to see them passing and passing
and going their own way,
especially if I see their aloneness alive in them.
Yet I don't want them to come near.
If they will only leave me alone
I can still have the illusion that there is room enough in the
world.

D. H. Lawrence

Conflict

from *Beowulf*

Then, on the headland, the Geats prepared a mighty pyre
for Beowulf, hung round with helmets and shields
and shining mail, in accordance with his wishes:
and then the mourning warriors laid
their dear lord, the famous prince, upon it.

And there on Whaleness, the heroes kindled
the most mighty of pyres; the dark wood-smoke
soared over the fire, the roaring flames
mingled with weeping – the wind's tumult subsided –
until the body became ash, consumed even
to its core. The heart's cup overflowed;
they mourned their loss, the death of their lord.
And, likewise, a maiden of the Geats,
with her tresses swept up, intoned
a dirge for Beowulf time after time,
declared she lived in dread of days to come
dark with carnage and keening terror of the enemy,
humiliation and captivity.
                                    Heaven swallowed the smoke.

Then the Geats built a barrow on the headland –
it was high and broad, visible from far
to all seafarers; in ten days they built the beacon
for that courageous man; and they constructed
as noble an enclosure as wise men
could devise, to enshrine the ashes.
They buried rings and brooches in the barrow,

all those adornments that brave men
had brought out from the hoard after Beowulf died.
They bequeathed the gleaming gold, treasure of men,
to the earth, and there it still remains
as useless to men as it was before.

    Then twelve brave warriors, sons of heroes,
rode round the barrow, sorrowing;
they mourned their king, chanted
an elegy, spoke about that great man:
they exalted his heroic life, lauded
his daring deeds; it is fitting for a man,
when his lord and friend must leave this life,
to mouth words in his praise
and to cherish his memory.
Thus the Geats, his hearth-companions,
grieved over the death of their lord;
they said that of all kings on earth
he was the kindest, the most gentle,
the most just to his people, the most eager for fame.

Anon.
[10th century] translated by Kevin Crossley-Holland

from Morte D'Arthur

Then quickly rose Sir Bedivere, and ran,
And, leaping down the ridges lightly, plunged
Among the bulrush beds, and clutch'd the sword,
And strongly wheel'd and threw it. The great brand

Made lightnings in the splendour of the moon,
And flashing round and round, and whirl'd in an arch,
Shot like a streamer of the northern morn,
Seen where the moving isles of winter shock
By night, with noises of the Northern Sea.
So flash'd and fell the brand Excalibur:
But ere he dipt the surface, rose an arm
Clothed in white samite, mystic, wonderful,
And caught him by the hilt, and brandish'd him
Three times, and drew him under in the mere.
And lightly went the other to the King.

Alfred, Lord Tennyson

Drake's Drum

Drake he's in his hammock an' a thousand mile away,
    (Capten, art tha sleepin' there below?),
Slung atween the round shot in Nombre Dios Bay,
    An' dreamin' arl the time o' Plymouth Hoe.
Yarnder lumes the Island, yarnder lie the ships,
    Wi' sailor lads a dancin' heel-an'-toe,
An' the shore-lights flashin', an' the night-tide dashin',
    He sees et arl so plainly as he saw et long ago.

Drake he was a Devon man, an' rüled the Devon seas,
    (Capten, art tha sleepin' there below?),
Rovin' tho' his death fell, he went wi' heart at ease,
    An' dreamin' arl the time o' Plymouth Hoe.
'Take my drum to England, hang et by the shore,
    Strike et when your powder's runnin' low;
If the Dons sight Devon, I'll quit the port o' Heaven,
    An' drum them up the Channel as we drummed them
      long ago.'

Drake he's in his hammock till the great Armadas come,
    (Capten, art tha sleepin' there below?),
Slung atween the round shot, listenin' for the drum,
    An' dreamin' arl the time o' Plymouth Hoe.
Call him on the deep sea, call him up the Sound,
    Call him when ye sail to meet the foe;
Where the old trade's plyin' an' the old flag flyin'
    They shall find him ware an' wakin', as they found him
      long ago!

Sir Henry Newbolt

The Destruction of Sennacherib

The Assyrian came down like the wolf on the fold,
And his cohorts were gleaming in purple and gold;
And the sheen of their spears was like stars on the sea,
When the blue wave rolls nightly on deep Galilee.

Like the leaves of the forest when Summer is green,
That host with their banners at sunset were seen:
Like the leaves of the forest when Autumn hath blown,
That host on the morrow lay wither'd and strown.

For the Angel of Death spread his wings on the blast,
And breathed in the face of the foe as he pass'd;
And the eyes of the sleepers wax'd deadly and chill,
And their hearts but once heaved, and for ever grew still!

And there lay the steed with his nostril all wide,
But through it there roll'd not the breath of his pride;
And the foam of his gasping lay white on the turf,
And cold as the spray of the rock-beating surf.

And there lay the rider distorted and pale,
With the dew on his brow, and the rust on his mail:
And the tents were all silent, the banner alone,
The lances unlifted, the trumpet unblown.

And the widows of Ashur are loud in their wail,
And the idols are broke in the temple of Baal;
And the might of the Gentile, unsmote by the sword,
Hath melted like snow in the glance of the Lord!

Lord Byron

Casabianca

The boy stood on the burning deck,
　　Whence all but he had fled;
The flame that lit the battle's wreck
　　Shone round him o'er the dead.

Yet beautiful and bright he stood,
　　As born to rule the storm;
A creature of heroic blood,
　　A proud though childlike form.

The flames rolled on; he would not go
　　Without his father's word;
That father, faint in death below,
　　His voice no longer heard.

He called aloud, 'Say, Father, say,
　　If yet my task be done!'
He knew not that the chieftain lay
　　Unconscious of his son.

'Speak, Father!' once again he cried,
　　'If I may yet be gone!'
And but the booming shots replied,
　　And fast the flames rolled on.

Upon his brow he felt their breath,
   And in his waving hair,
And looked from that lone post of death
   In still yet brave despair;

And shouted but once more aloud,
   'My Father! must I stay?'
While o'er him fast, through sail and shroud,
   The wreathing fires made way.

They wrapped the ship in splendour wild,
   They caught the flag on high,
And streamed above the gallant child,
   Like banners in the sky.

There came a burst of thunder sound;
   The boy – Oh! where was he?
Ask of the winds, that far around
   With fragments strewed the sea –

With mast and helm and pennon fair,
   That well had borne their part –
But the noblest thing that perished there
   Was that young, faithful heart.

Felicia D. Hemans

The Burial of Sir John Moore
After Corunna

Not a drum was heard, not a funeral note,
  As his corse to the rampart we hurried;
Not a soldier discharged his farewell shot
  O'er the grave where our hero we buried.

We buried him darkly at dead of night,
  The sods with our bayonets turning,
By the struggling moonbeam's misty light
  And the lanthorn dimly burning.

No useless coffin enclosed his breast,
  Not in sheet or in shroud we wound him;
But he lay like a warrior taking his rest
  With his martial cloak around him.

Few and short were the prayers we said
  And we spoke not a word of sorrow;
But we steadfastly gazed on the face that was dead,
  And we bitterly thought of the morrow

We thought, as we hollow'd his narrow bed
  And smooth'd down his lowly pillow,
That the foe and the stranger would tread o'er his head,
  And we far away on the billow!

Lightly they'll talk of the spirit that's gone,
   And o'er his cold ashes upbraid him –
But little he'll reck, if they let him sleep on
   In the grave where a Briton has laid him.

But half of our heavy task was done
   When the clock struck the hour for retiring:
And we heard the distant and random gun
   That the foe was sullenly firing.

Slowly and sadly we laid him down,
   From the field of his fame fresh and gory;
We carved not a line, and we raised not a stone,
   But we left him alone with his glory.

Charles Wolfe

The Charge of the Light Brigade

Half a league, half a league,
   Half a league onward,
All in the valley of Death
   Rode the six hundred.
'Forward, the Light Brigade!
Charge for the guns!' he said:
Into the valley of Death
   Rode the six hundred.

'Forward, the Light Brigade!'
Was there a man dismay'd?
Not tho' the soldier knew
Someone had blunder'd:
Theirs not to make reply,
Theirs not to reason why,
Theirs but to do and die:
Into the valley of Death
Rode the six hundred.

Cannon to right of them,
Cannon to left of them,
Cannon in front of them
Volley'd and thunder'd;
Storm'd at with shot and shell,
Boldly they rode and well,
Into the jaws of Death,
Into the mouth of Hell
Rode the six hundred.

Flash'd all their sabres bare,
Flash'd as they turn'd in air
Sabring the gunners there,
Charging an army, while
All the world wonder'd:
Plunged in the battery-smoke
Right thro' the line they broke;
Cossack and Russian
Reel'd from the sabre-stroke
Shatter'd and sunder'd.

Then they rode back, but not
Not the six hundred.
Cannon to right of them,
Cannon to left of them;
Cannon behind them
Volley'd and thunder'd;
Storm'd at with shot and shell,
While horse and hero fell,
They that had fought so well
Came thro' the jaws of Death,
Back from the mouth of Hell,
All that was left of them.
Left of six hundred.

When can their glory fade?
O the wild charge they made!
All the world wonder'd.
Honour the charge they made!
Honour the Light Brigade,
Noble six hundred!

Alfred, Lord Tennyson

In Flanders Fields

In Flanders fields the poppies blow
Between the crosses, row on row,
   That mark our place; and in the sky
   The larks, still bravely singing, fly
Scarce heard amid the guns below.

We are the Dead. Short days ago
We lived, felt dawn, saw sunset glow,
   Loved and were loved, and now we lie
   In Flanders fields.

Take up our quarrel with the foe:
To you from failing hands we throw
   The torch; be yours to hold it high.
   If ye break faith with us who die
We shall not sleep, though poppies grow
   In Flanders fields.

John McCrae

Magic and Mystery

The Dark House

In a dark, dark wood, there was a dark, dark house,
And in that dark, dark house, there was a dark, dark
    room,
And in that dark, dark room, there was a dark, dark
    cupboard,
And in that dark, dark cupboard, there was a dark, dark
    shelf,
And in that dark, dark shelf, there was a dark, dark box,
And in that dark, dark box, there was a GHOST!

Anon.

The Deserted House

There's no smoke in the chimney,
    And the rain beats on the floor;
There's no glass in the window,
    There's no wood in the door;
The heather grows behind the house,
    And the sand lies before.

No hand hath trained the ivy,
 The walls are grey and bare;
The boats upon the sea sail by,
 Nor ever tarry there.
No beast of the field comes nigh,
 Nor any bird of the air.

     Mary Coleridge

Overheard on a Saltmarsh

Nymph, nymph, what are your beads?

Green glass, goblin. Why do you stare at them?

Give them me.

    No.

Give them me. Give them me.

      No.

Then I will howl all night in the reeds,
Lie in the mud and howl for them.

Goblin, why do you love them so?

They are better than stars or water,
Better than voices of winds that sing,
Better than any man's fair daughter,
Your green glass beads on a silver ring.

Hush, I stole them out of the moon.

Give me your beads, I want them.

          No.

I will howl in a deep lagoon
For your green glass beads, I love them so.
Give them me. Give them.

          No.

Harold Monro

The Listeners

'Is there anybody there?' said the Traveller,
  Knocking on the moonlit door;
And his horse in the silence champed the grasses
  Of the forest's ferny floor.
And a bird flew up out of the turret,
  Above the Traveller's head:
And he smote upon the door a second time;
  'Is there anybody there?' he said.

But no one descended to the Traveller;
　No head from the leaf-fringed sill
Leaned over and looked into his grey eyes,
　Where he stood perplexed and still.
But only a host of phantom listeners
　That dwelt in the lone house then
Stood listening in the quiet of the moonlight
　To that voice from the world of men:
Stood thronging the faint moonbeams on the dark stair,
　That goes down to the empty hall,
Hearkening in an air stirred and shaken
　By the lonely Traveller's call.
And he felt in his heart their strangeness,
　Their stillness answering his cry,
While his horse moved, cropping the dark turf,
　'Neath the starred and leafy sky;
For he suddenly smote on the door, even
　Louder, and lifted his head: –
'Tell them I came, and no one answered
　That I kept my word,' he said.
Never the least stir made the listeners,
　Though every word he spake
Fell echoing through the shadowiness of the still house
　From the one man left awake:
Ay, they heard his foot upon the stirrup,
　And the sound of iron on stone,
And how the silence surged softly backward,
　When the plunging hoofs were gone.

Walter de la Mare

The Man Who Wasn't There

As I was going up the stair
I met a man who wasn't there.
He wasn't there again today –
Oh, how I wish he'd go away!

Anon.

Mr Nobody

I know a funny little man,
   As quiet as a mouse.
He does the mischief that is done
   In everybody's house.
Though no one ever sees his face,
   Yet one and all agree
That every plate we break, was cracked
   By Mr Nobody.

'Tis he who always tears our books,
   Who leaves the door ajar.
He picks the buttons from our shirts,
   And scatters pins afar.
That squeaking door will always squeak –
   For prithee, don't you see?
We leave the oiling to be done
   By Mr Nobody.

He puts damp wood upon the fire,
   That kettles will not boil:
His are the feet that bring in mud
   And all the carpets soil.
The papers that so oft are lost –
   Who had them last but he?
There's no one tosses them about
   But Mr Nobody.

The fingermarks upon the door
   By none of us were made.
We never leave the blinds unclosed
   To let the curtains fade.
The ink we never spill! The boots
   That lying round you see,
Are not our boots – they all belong
   To Mr Nobody.

Anon.

The Visitor

A crumbling churchyard, the sea and the moon;
The waves had gouged out grave and bone;
A man was walking, late and alone . . .

He saw a skeleton white on the ground,
A ring on a bony hand he found.

He ran home to his wife and gave her the ring.
'Oh, where did you get it?' He said not a thing.

'It's the prettiest ring in the world,' she said,
As it glowed on her finger. They skipped off to bed.

At midnight they woke. In the dark outside,
'Give me my ring!' a chill voice cried.

'What was that, William? What did it say?'
'Don't worry, my dear. It'll soon go away.'

'I'm coming!' A skeleton opened the door.
'Give me my ring!' It was crossing the floor.

'What was that, William? What did it say?'
'Don't worry, my dear. It'll soon go away.'

'I'm touching you now! I'm climbing the bed.'
The wife pulled the sheet right over her head.

It was torn from her grasp and tossed in the air:
'I'll drag you out of your bed by the hair!'

'What was that, William? What did it say?'
'Throw the ring through the window! THROW IT AWAY!'

She threw it. The skeleton leapt from the sill,
Scooped up the ring and clattered downhill,
Fainter . . . and fainter . . . Then all was still.

Ian Serraillier

The Ghosts' High Noon

When the night wind howls in the chimney cowls, and
    the bat in the moonlight flies,
And inky clouds, like funeral shrouds, sail over the
    midnight skies –
When the footpads quail at the night-bird's wail, and black
    dogs bay the moon,
Then is the spectres' holiday – then is the ghosts' high noon!

As the sob of the breeze sweeps over the trees, and the
    mists lie low on the fen,
From grey tombstones are gathered the bones that once
    were women and men,
And away they go, with a mop and a mow, to the revel
    that ends too soon,
For cockcrow limits our holiday – the dead of the night's
    high noon!

And then each ghost with his ladye-toast to their
    churchyard beds take flight,
With a kiss, perhaps, on her lantern chaps, and a grisly
    grim 'good night';
Till the welcome knell of the midnight bell rings forth its
    jolliest tune,
And ushers our next high holiday – the dead of the night's
    high noon!

W. S. Gilbert

Eldorado

Gaily bedight,
A gallant knight,
In sunshine and in shadow,
Had journeyed long,
Singing a song,
In search of Eldorado.

But he grew old –
This knight so bold –
And o'er his heart a shadow
Fell as he found
No spot of ground
That looked like Eldorado.

And, as his strength
Failed him at length,
He met a pilgrim shadow:
'Shadow,' said he,
'Where can it be,
This land of Eldorado?'

'Over the mountains
Of the Moon,
Down the valley of the Shadow,
Ride, boldly ride,'
The shade replied,
'If you seek for Eldorado.'

Edgar Allan Poe

Kubla Khan

In Xanadu did Kubla Khan
A stately pleasure-dome decree:
Where Alph, the sacred river, ran
Through caverns measureless to man
Down to a sunless sea.
So twice five miles of fertile ground
With walls and towers were girdled round:
And there were gardens bright with sinuous rills
Where blossom'd many an incense-bearing tree;
And here were forests ancient as the hills,
Enfolding sunny spots of greenery.

But O, that deep romantic chasm which slanted
Down the green hill athwart a cedarn cover!
A savage place! as holy and enchanted
As e'er beneath a waning moon was haunted
By woman wailing for her demon-lover!
And from this chasm, with ceaseless turmoil seething,
As if this earth in fast thick pants were breathing,
A mighty fountain momently was forced;
Amid whose swift half-intermitted burst
Huge fragments vaulted like rebounding hail,
Or chaffy grain beneath the thresher's flail:
And 'mid these dancing rocks at once and ever
It flung up momently the sacred river.
Five miles meandering with a mazy motion
Through wood and dale the sacred river ran,
Then reach'd the caverns measureless to man,

And sank in tumult to a lifeless ocean:
And 'mid this tumult Kubla heard from far
Ancestral voices prophesying war!
    The shadow of the dome of pleasure
        Floated midway on the waves;
    Where was heard the mingled measure
        From the fountain and the caves.
It was a miracle of rare device,
A sunny pleasure dome with caves of ice!

    A damsel with a dulcimer
        In a vision once I saw:
    It was an Abyssinian maid,
        And on her dulcimer she play'd,
    Singing of Mount Abora.
    Could I revive within me
    Her symphony and song,
To such a deep delight 'twould win me,
That with music loud and long,
I would build that dome in air,
That sunny dome! those caves of ice!
And all who heard should see them there,
And all should cry, Beware! Beware!
His flashing eyes, his floating hair!
Weave a circle round him thrice,
    And close your eyes with holy dread,
    For he on honey-dew hath fed,
And drunk the milk of Paradise.

Samuel Taylor Coleridge

from *A Midsummer Night's Dream*
Act II scene ii

You spotted snakes with double tongue,
   Thorny hedgehogs be not seen;
Newts and blindworms, do no wrong;
   Come not near our Fairy Queen.

    Philomel with melody,
    Sing in our sweet lullaby;
Lulla, lulla, lullaby; lulla, lulla, lullaby.
    Never harm
    Nor spell nor charm
  Come our lovely lady nigh.
So good night, with lullaby.

Weaving spiders, come not here;
   Hence, you long-legged spinners, hence;
Beetles black, approach not near;
   Worm nor snail do no offence.

    Philomel with melody,
    Sing in our sweet lullaby;
Lulla, lulla, lullaby; lulla, lulla, lullaby.
    Never harm
    Nor spell nor charm
  Come our lovely lady nigh.
So good night, with lullaby.

William Shakespeare

from *Macbeth*
Act IV scene ii

Round about the cauldron go:
In the poisoned entrails throw.
Toad, that under cold stone
Days and nights has thirty-one
Sweated venom sleeping got,
Boil thou first in the charmèd pot.
　　Double, double toil and trouble;
　　Fire burn and cauldron bubble.

Fillet of a fenny snake,
In the cauldron boil and bake;
Eye of newt and toe of frog,
Wool of bat and tongue of dog,
Adder's fork and blindworm's sting,
Lizard's leg and owlet's wing.
For a charm of powerful trouble,
Like a hell-broth boil and bubble.
　　Double, double toil and trouble;
　　Fire burn and cauldron bubble.

Scale of dragon, tooth of wolf,
Witch's mummy, maw and gulf
Of the ravenous salt-sea shark,
Root of hemlock digged in the dark,
Make the gruel thick and slab:
Add thereto a tiger's chaudron,
For the ingredients of our cauldron.
  Double, double toil and trouble,
  Fire burn and cauldron bubble.

William Shakespeare

The Hairy Toe

Once there was a woman went out to pick beans,
and she found a Hairy Toe.
She took the Hairy Toe home with her,
and that night, when she went to bed,
the wind began to moan and groan.
Away off in the distance
she seemed to hear a voice crying,
'Where's my Hair-r-ry To-o-oe?
Who's got my Hair-r-ry To-o-oe?'

The woman scrooched down,
'way down under the covers,
and about that time
the wind appeared to hit the house,

smoosh,

244

and the old house creaked and cracked
like something was trying to get in.
The voice had come nearer,
almost at the door now,
and it said,
'Where's my Hair-r-ry To-o-oe?
Who's got my Hair-r-ry To-o-oe?'

The woman scrooched further down
under the covers
and pulled them tight around her head.

The wind growled around the house
like some big animal
and r-r-um-mbled
over the chimbley.
All at once she heard the door cr-r-a-ack
and Something slipped in
and began to creep over the floor.

The floor went
cre-e-eak, cre-e-eak
at every step that thing took towards her bed.
The woman could almost feel
it bending over her bed.
There in an awful voice it said:
'Where's my Hair-r-ry To-o-oe?
Who's got my Hair-r-ry To-o-oe?
You've got it!'

Anon.

from *Haunted Houses*

All houses wherein men have lived and died
  Are haunted houses. Through the open doors
The harmless phantoms on their errands glide,
  With feet that make no sound upon the floors.

We meet them at the doorway, on the stair,
  Along the passages they come and go,
Impalpable impressions on the air,
  A sense of something moving to and fro.

There are more guests at the table than the hosts
  Invited; the illuminated hall
Is thronged with quiet, inoffensive ghosts,
  As silent as the pictures on the wall.

The stranger at my fireside cannot see
  The forms I see, nor hear the sounds I hear;
He but perceives what is; while unto me
  All that has been is visible and clear.

Henry Wadsworth Longfellow

Colours

Colours

What is pink?
A rose is pink
By the fountain's brink.

What is red?
A poppy's red
In its barley bed.

What is blue?
The sky is blue
Where the clouds float through.

What is white?
A swan is white
Sailing in the light.

What is yellow?
Pears are yellow,
Rich and ripe and mellow.

What is green?
The grass is green
With small flowers between.

What is violet?
Clouds are violet
In the summer twilight.

What is orange?
Why, an orange,
Just an orange!

Christina Rossetti

The Colour

*(The following lines are partly original, partly remembered
from a Wessex folk-rhyme)*

'What shall I bring you?
Please will white do
Best for your wearing
The long day through?'
'– White is for weddings,
Weddings, weddings,
White is for weddings,
And that won't do.'

'What shall I bring you?
Please will red do
The long day through?'
'– Red is for soldiers,
Soldiers, soldiers
Red is for soldiers
And that won't do.'

'What shall I bring you?
Please will blue do
Best for your wearing
The long day through?'
'– Blue is for sailors
Sailors, sailors
Blue is for sailors
And that won't do.'

'What shall I bring you?
Please will green do
Best for your wearing
The long day through?'
'– Green is for mayings.
Mayings, mayings
Green is for mayings,
And that won't do.'

'What shall I bring you
Then? Will black do
Best for your wearing
The long day through?'
'– Black is for mourning,
Mourning, mourning,
Black is for mourning,
And black will do.'

Thomas Hardy

The Paint Box

'Cobalt and umber and ultramarine,
Ivory black and emerald green –
What shall I paint to give pleasure to you?'
'Paint for me somebody utterly new.'

'I have painted you tigers in crimson and white.'
'The colours were good and you painted aright.'
'I have painted the cook and a camel in blue
And a panther in purple.' 'You painted them true.

Now mix me a colour that nobody knows,
And paint me a country where nobody goes,
And put in it people a little like you,
Watching a unicorn drinking the dew.'

E. V. Rieu

Colours

Red is death, for people who are dying,
Silver is tears, for people who are crying,
Blue is a pool, cool and still,
Green is a beautiful grassy hill.

Grey is for people in the early evening,
Black is a dress for people grieving,
Brown is for an old queen's gown,
Gold for a princess's crown.

Frances Evans

Silver

Slowly, silently, now the moon
Walks the night in her silver shoon;
This way and that, she peers, and sees
Silver fruit upon silver trees;
One by one the casements catch
Her beams beneath the silvery tharch;
Couched in his kennel, like a log,
With paws of silver sleeps the dog;
From their shadowy cote the white breasts peep
Of doves in a silver-feathered sleep;
A harvest mouse goes scampering by,
With silver claws, and silver eye;
And moveless fish in the water gleam,
By silver reeds in a silver stream.

Walter de la Mare

I Asked the Little Boy Who Cannot See

I asked the little boy who cannot see,
'And what is colour like?'
'Why, green,' said he,
'Is like the rustle when the wind blows through
The forest; running water, that is blue;
And red is like a trumpet sound; and pink
Is like the smell of roses; and I think
That purple must be like a thunderstorm;
And yellow is like something soft and warm;
And white is a pleasant stillness when you lie and dream.'

Anon.

from *Sing-Song*

An emerald is as green as grass;
A ruby red as blood;
A sapphire shines as blue as heaven;
A flint lies in the mud.

A diamond is a brilliant stone,
To catch the world's desire;
An opal holds a fiery spark;
But a flint holds fire.

Christina Rossetti

Nonsense Poems

The Sad Story of a Little Boy That Cried

Once a little boy, Jack, was, oh! ever so good,
Till he took a strange notion to cry all he could.

So he cried all the day, and he cried all the night,
He cried in the morning, and in the twilight;

He cried till his voice was as hoarse as a crow,
And his mouth grew so large it looked like a great O.

It grew at the bottom, and grew at the top;
It grew till they thought that it never would stop.

Each day his great mouth grew taller and taller,
And his dear little self grew smaller and smaller.

At last, that same mouth grew so big that – alack! –
It was only a mouth with a border of Jack.

Anon.

Imagine

If the sea was in the sky,
And trees grew underground,
And if all fish had giant teeth,
And all the cows were round;
If birds flew backwards all the time,
And vultures ruled the land;
If bricks poured down instead of rain,
If all there was was sand;
If every man had seven heads
And we spoke Double Dutch,
And if the sun came out at night,
I wouldn't like it much.

Anon.

The Jumblies

They went to sea in a Sieve, they did,
    In a Sieve they went to sea;
In spite of all their friends could say,
On a winter's morn, on a stormy day,
    In a Sieve they went to sea!
And when the Sieve turned round and round
And everyone cried, 'You'll all be drowned!'
They cried aloud, 'Our Sieve ain't big,

But we don't care a button, we don't care a fig!
    In a Sieve we'll go to sea!'
Far and few, far and few,
    Are the lands where the Jumblies live;
Their heads are green and their hands are blue,
    And they went to sea in a Sieve.

They sailed away in a Sieve, they did,
    In a Sieve they sailed so fast,
With only a beautiful pea-green veil
Tied with a riband, by way of a sail,
    To a small tobacco-pipe mast:
And everyone said who saw them go,
'Oh, won't they be soon upset, you know!
For the sky is dark, and the voyage is long,
And happen what may, it's extremely wrong
    In a Sieve to sail so fast!'

The water it soon came in, it did,
    The water it soon came in;
So to keep them dry they wrapped their feet
In a pinky paper all folded neat,
    And they fastened it down with a pin.
And they passed the night in a crockery jar,
And each of them said, 'How wise we are!
Though the sky be dark, and the voyage be long,
Yet we never can think we were rash or wrong
    While round in our Sieve we spin!'

And all night long they sailed away;
    And when the sun went down
They whistled and warbled a moony song,
The echoing sound of a coppery gong,
    In the shade of the mountains brown.
'O Timballo! How happy we are
When we live in a Sieve and a crockery jar,
And all night long in the moonlight pale
We sail away with a pea-green veil
    In the shade of the mountains brown!'

They sailed to the Western Sea, they did,
    To a land all covered with trees,
And they bought an Owl, and a useful Cart,
And a pound of Rice, and a Cranberry Tart,
    And a hive of Silvery Bees.
And they bought a Pig, and some green Jackdaws,
And a lovely Monkey with lollipop paws,
And forty bottles of Ring-Bo-Ree,
    And no end of Stilton Cheese.

And in twenty years they all came back,
    In twenty years or more,
And everyone said, 'How tall they've grown!
For they've been to the Lakes, and the Torrible Zone,
    And the hills of the Chankly Bore!'
And they drank their health, and gave them a feast
Of dumplings made of beautiful yeast;
And everyone said, 'If we only live,

We, too, will go to sea in a Sieve –
   To the hills of the Chankly Bore!'
Far and few, far and few,
   Are the lands where the Jumblies live;
Their heads are green and their hands are blue,
   And they went to sea in a Sieve.

Edward Lear

The Owl And The Pussy-Cat

The Owl and the Pussy-Cat went to sea
   In a beautiful pea-green boat,
They took some honey, and plenty of money,
   Wrapped up in a five-pound note.
The Owl looked up to the stars above,
   And sang to a small guitar,
'O lovely Pussy! O Pussy, my love,
   What a beautiful Pussy you are,
     You are,
     You are!
   What a beautiful Pussy you are!'

Pussy said to the Owl, 'You elegant fowl!
   How charmingly sweet you sing!
O let us be married! too long we have tarried
   But what shall we do for a ring?'

They sailed away for a year and a day,
    To the land where the Bong-tree grows,
And there in a wood a Piggy-wig stood,
    With a ring at the end of his nose,
      His nose,
      His nose,
    With a ring at the end of his nose.

'Dear Pig, are you willing to sell for one shilling
    Your ring?' Said the Piggy, 'I will.'
So they took it away, and were married next day
    By the Turkey who lives on the hill.
They dined on mince, and slices of quince,
    Which they ate with a runcible spoon;
And hand in hand, on the edge of the sand,
    They danced by the light of the moon,
      The moon,
      The moon,
    They danced by the light of the moon.

Edward Lear

A Quadrupedremian Song

He dreamt that he saw the Buffalant,
And the spottified Dromedaraffe.
The blue Camelotamus, lean and gaunt,
And the wild Tigeroceros calf.

262

The maned Liodillo loudly roared,
And the Peccarbok whistled its whine,
The Chinchayak leapt on the dewy sward,
As it hunted the pale Baboopine.

He dreamt that he met the Crocoghau,
As it swam in the Stagnolent Lake;
But everything that in dreams he saw
Came of eating too freely of cake.

Thomas Hood

The Man in the Wilderness

The man in the wilderness asked of me,
How many strawberries grew in the sea?
I answered him as I thought good
As many red herrings as grew in a wood.

Anon.

There Was an Old Man

There was an Old Man with a beard,
Who said, 'It is just as I feared! –
Two owls and a hen,
Four larks and a wren,
Have all built their nests in my beard!'

Edward Lear

You Are Old, Father William

'You are old, Father William,' the young man said,
    'And your hair has become very white;
And yet you incessantly stand on your head –
    Do you think, at your age, it is right?'

'In my youth,' Father William replied to his son,
    'I feared it might injure the brain;
But now that I'm perfectly sure I have none,
    Why, I do it again and again.'

'You are old,' said the youth, 'as I mentioned before,
    And have grown most uncommonly fat;
Yet you turned a back-somersault in at the door –
    Pray, what is the reason of that?'

'In my youth,' said the sage, as he shook his grey locks,
  'I kept all my limbs very supple
By the use of this ointment – one shilling the box –
  Allow me to sell you a couple.'

'You are old,' said the youth, 'and your jaws are too weak
  For anything tougher than suet;
Yet you finished the goose, with the bones and the beak –
  Pray, how did you manage to do it?'

'In my youth,' said his father, 'I took to the law,
  And argued each case with my wife;
And the muscular strength which it gave to my jaw
  Has lasted the rest of my life.'

'You are old,' said the youth; 'one would hardly suppose
  That your eye was as steady as ever;
Yet you balanced an eel on the end of your nose –
  What made you so awfully clever?'

'I have answered three questions, and that is enough,'
  Said his father; 'don't give yourself airs!
Do you think I can listen all day to such stuff?
  Be off, or I'll kick you down stairs!'

Lewis Carroll

Jabberwocky

'Twas brillig, and the slithy toves
    Did gyre and gimble in the wabe:
All mimsy were the borogoves,
    And the mome raths outgrabe.

'Beware the Jabberwock, my son!
    The jaws that bite, the claws that catch!
Beware the Jubjub bird, and shun
    The frumious Bandersnatch!'

He took his vorpal sword in hand:
    Long time the manxome foe he sought –
So rested he by the Tumtum tree,
    And stood awhile in thought.

And as in uffish thought he stood,
    The Jabberwock, with eyes of flame,
Came whiffling through the tulgey wood,
    And burbled as it came!

One, two! One, two! And through and through
    The vorpal blade went snicker-snack!
He left it dead, and with its head
    He went galumphing back.

'And hast thou slain the Jabberwock?
    Come to my arms, my beamish boy!
O frabjous day! Callooh! Callay!'
    He chortled in his joy.

'Twas brillig, and the slithy toves
    Did gyre and gimble in the wabe:
All mimsy were the borogoves,
    And the mome raths outgrabe.

Lewis Carroll

I went to the pictures tomorrow

I went to the pictures tomorrow
And took a front seat at the back
I fell from the pit to the gallery
And broke a front bone in my back
The lady she gave me some chocolate
I ate it and gave it her back
I phoned for a taxi and walked it
And that's why I never came back

Anon.

Modern Classics

The Door

Go and open the door.
Maybe outside there's
a tree, or a wood,
a garden,
or a magic city.

Go and open the door.
Maybe a dog's rummaging.
Maybe you'll see a face,
or an eye,
or the picture
of a picture.

Go and open the door.
If there's a fog
it will clear.

Go and open the door.
Even if there's only
the darkness ticking,
even if there's only
the hollow wind,
even if
nothing
is there,
go and open the door.

At least
there'll be
a draught.

Miroslav Holub

The Magic Box

I will put in the box

the swish of a silk sari on a summer night,
fire from the nostrils of a Chinese dragon,
the tip of a tongue touching a tooth.

I will put in the box

a snowman with a rumbling belly,
a sip of the bluest water from Lake Lucerne,
a leaping spark from an electric fish.

I will put in the box

three violet wishes spoken in Gujarati,
the last joke of an ancient uncle
and the first smile of a baby.

I will put in the box

a fifth season and a black sun,
a cowboy on a broomstick
and a witch on a white horse.

My box is fashioned from ice and gold and steel,
with stars on the lid and secrets in the corners.
Its hinges are the toe joints
of dinosaurs.

I shall surf on my box
on the great high-rolling breakers of the wild Atlantic,
then wash ashore on a yellow beach
the colour of the sun.

Kit Wright

My Mother Saw a Dancing Bear

My mother saw a dancing bear
By the schoolyard, a day in June.
The keeper stood with chain and bar
And whistle-pipe, and played a tune.

And bruin lifted up its head
And lifted up its dusty feet,
And all the children laughed to see
It caper in the summer heat.

They watched as for the Queen it died.
They watched it march. They watched it halt.
They heard the keeper as he cried,
'Now, roly-poly!' 'Somersault!'

And then, my mother said, there came
The keeper with a begging-cup.
The bear with burning coat of fur,
Shaming the laughter to a stop.

They paid a penny for the dance,
But what they saw was not the show;
Only, in Bruin's aching eyes,
Far-distant forests, and the snow.

Charles Causley

Colonel Fazackerley

Colonel Fazackerley Butterworth-Toast
Bought an old castle complete with a ghost,
But someone or other forgot to declare
To Colonel Fazack that the spectre was there.

On the very first evening, while waiting to dine,
The Colonel was taking a fine sherry wine,
When the ghost, with a furious flash and a flare,
Shot out of the chimney and shivered, 'Beware!'

Colonel Fazackerley put down his glass
And said, 'My dear fellow, that's really first class!
I just can't conceive how you do it at all.
I imagine you're going to a Fancy Dress Ball?'

At this, the dread ghost gave a withering cry.
Said the Colonel (his monocle firm in his eye),
'Now just how you do it I wish I could think.
Do sit down and tell me, and please have a drink.'

The ghost in his phosphorous cloak gave a roar
And floated about between ceiling and floor.
He walked through a wall and returned through a pane
And backed up the chinney and came down again.

Said the Colonel, 'With laughter I'm feeling quite weak!'
(As trickles of merriment ran down his cheek)
'My house-warming party I hope you won't spurn
You *must* say you'll come and you'll give us a turn!'

At this, the poor spectre – quite out of his wits –
Proceeded to shake himself almost to bits.
He rattled his chains and he clattered his bones
And he filled the whole castle with mumbles and moans.

But Colonel Fazackerley, just as before,
Was simply delighted and called out, 'Encore!'
At which the ghost vanished, his efforts in vain,
And never was seen at the castle again.

'Oh dear, what a pity!' said Colonel Fazack.
'I don't know his name, so I can't call him back.'
And then with a smile that was hard to define,
Colonel Fazackerley went in to dine.

Charles Causley

The Marrog

My desk's at the back of the class
And nobody nobody knows
I'm a Marrog from Mars
With a body of brass
And seventeen fingers and toes.
Wouldn't they shriek if they knew
I've three eyes at the back of my head
And my hair is bright purple
My nose is deep blue
And my teeth are half yellow half red?
My five arms are silver with knives on them sharper than
    spears.
I could go back right now if I liked –
And return in a million light years.
I could gobble them all for
I'm seven foot tall
And I'm breathing green flames from my ears.
Wouldn't they yell if they knew
If they guessed that a Marrog was here?

Ha-ha they haven't a clue –
Or wouldn't they tremble with fear!
Look, look, a Marrog
They'd all scrum and shout.
The blackboard would fall and the ceiling would crack
And the teacher would faint I suppose.
But I grin to myself sitting right at the back
And Nobody nobody knows.

R. C. Scriven

Dog *in the Playground*

Dog in the playground
Suddenly there.
Smile on his face,
Tail in the air.

Dog in the playground
Bit of a fuss:
I know that dog –
Lives next to us!

Dog in the playground:
Oh, no he don't.
He'll come with me,
You see if he won't.

The word gets round;
The crowd gets bigger.
His name's Bob.
It ain't – it's Trigger.

They call him Archie!
They call him Frank!
Lives by the Fish Shop!
Lives up the Bank!
Who told you that?
Pipe down! Shut up!
I know that dog
Since he was a pup.

Dog in the playground:
We'll catch him, Miss.
Leave it to us.
Just watch this!

Dog in the playground
What a to-do!
Thirty-five children,
Caretaker too,
Chasing the dog,
Chasing each other.
I know that dog –
He's our dog's brother!

We've cornered him now;
He can't get away.
Told you we'd catch him,
Robert and – Hey!
Don't open that door –
Oh, Glenis, you fool!
Look, Miss, what's happened:
Dog in the school.

Dog in the classroom,
Dog in the hall,
Dog in the toilets –
He's paying a call!
Forty-six children,
Caretaker too,
Headmaster, three teachers,
Hullabaloo!

Lost him! Can't find him!
He's vanished! And then:
Look, Miss, he's back
In the playground again.

Shouting and shoving –
I'll give you what for! –
Sixty-five children
Head for the door.

Dog in the playground,
Smile on his face,
Tail in the air,
Winning the race.

Dog in his element
Off at a jog,
Out of the gates:
Wish I was a dog.

Dog in the playground:
Couldn't he run?

Dog in the playground
. . . Gone!

Alan Ahlberg

Chocolate Cake

I love chocolate cake.
And when I was a boy
I loved it even more.

Sometimes we used to have it for tea
and Mum used to say,
'If there's any left over
you can have it to take to school
tomorrow to have at playtime.'
And the next day I would take it to school

wrapped up in tin foil
open it up at playtime and sit in the
corner of the playground
eating it,
you know how the icing on top
is all shiny and it cracks as you
bite into it
and there's that other kind of icing in
the middle
and it sticks to your hands and you
can lick your fingers
and lick your lips
oh it's lovely.
Yeah.

Anyway,
once we had this chocolate cake for tea
and later I went to bed
but while I was in bed
I found myself waking up
licking my lips
and smiling.
I woke up proper.
'The chocolate cake.'
It was the first thing
I thought of.
I could almost see it
so I thought,
what if I go downstairs
and have a little nibble, yeah?

It was all dark
everyone was in bed
so it must have been really late
but I got out of bed,
crept out of the door

there's always a creaky floorboard, isn't there?

Past Mum and Dad's room,

careful not to tread on bits of broken toys
or bits of Lego
you know what it's like treading on Lego
with your bare feet,

yowwww
shhhhhhh

downstairs
into the kitchen
open the cupboard
and there it is
all shining.

So I take it out of the cupboard
put it on the table
and I see that
there's a few crumbs lying about on the plate,
so I lick my finger and run my finger all over the crumbs
scooping them up
and put them into my mouth.

ooooooooommmmmmmmm

nice.

Then
I look again
and on one side where it's been cut,
it's all crumbly.
So I take a knife
I think I'll just tidy that up a bit,
cut off the crumbly bits
scoop them all up
and into the mouth

oooooommm   mmmm
nice.

Look at the cake again.

That looks a bit funny now,
one side doesn't match the other
I'll just even it up a bit, eh?

Take the knife
and slice.
This time the knife makes a little cracky noise
as it goes through that hard icing on top.

A whole slice this time,

into the mouth.

Oh the icing on top
and the icing in the middle
ohhhhhh oooo mmmmmm.

But now
I can't stop myself.
Knife –
I just take any old slice at it
and I've got this great big chunk
and I'm cramming it in
what a greedy pig
but it's so nice,

and there's another
and another and I'm squealing and I'm smacking my lips
and I'm stuffing myself with it
and
before I know
I've eaten the lot.
The whole lot.
I look at the plate.
It's all gone.

Oh no
they're bound to notice, aren't they,
a whole chocolate cake doesn't just disappear
does it?

What shall I do?

I know, I'll wash the plate up,
and the knife

and put them away and maybe no one
will notice, eh?

So I do that
and creep creep creep
back to bed
into bed
doze off
licking my lips
with a lovely feeling in my belly.
Mmmmmmmmmmm.

In the morning I get up,
downstairs,
have breakfast,
Mum's saying,
'Have you got your dinner money?'
and I say,
'Yes.'
'And don't forget to take some chocolate cake with you.'
I stopped breathing.

'What's the matter,' she says,
'you normally jump at chocolate cake?'

I'm still not breathing,
and she's looking at me very closely now.
She's looking at me just below my mouth.
'What's that?' she says.
'What's what?' I say.
'What's that there?'
'Where?'
'There,' she says, pointing at my chin.
'I don't know,' I say.
'It looks like chocolate,' she says.
'It's not chocolate cake is it?'
No answer.
'Is it?'
'I don't know.'
She goes to the cupboard
looks in, up, top, middle, bottom,
turns back to me.
It's gone.
It's gone.
'You haven't eaten it, have you?'
'I don't know.'
'You don't know? You don't know if you've eaten a whole
    chocolate cake or not?
'When? When did you eat it?'

So I told her,

and she said
well what could she say?
'That's the last time I give you any cake to take to school.
Now go. Get out
no wait
not before you've washed your dirty sticky face.'
I went upstairs
looked in the mirror
and there it was,
just below my mouth,
a chocolate smudge.
The give-away.
Maybe she'll forget about it by next week.

Michael Rosen

The Cats' Protection League

Midnight. A knock at the door.
Open it? Better had.
Three heavy cats, mean and bad.

They offer protection. I ask, 'What for?'
The Boss-cat snarls, 'You know the score.
Listen man and listen good

If you wanna stay in the neighbourhood,
Pay your dues or the toms will call
And wail each night on the backyard wall.

Mangle the flowers, and as for the lawn
A smelly minefield awaits you at dawn.'
These guys meant business without a doubt

Three cans of tuna, I handed them out.
They then disappeared like bats into hell
Those bad, bad cats from the CPL.

Roger McGough

Hide and Seek

Call out. Call loud: 'I'm ready! Come and find me!'
The sacks in the toolshed smell like the seaside.
They'll never find you in this salty dark,
But be careful that your feet aren't sticking out.
Wiser not to risk another shout.
The floor is cold. They'll probably be searching
The bushes near the swing. Whatever happens
You mustn't sneeze when they come prowling in.
And here they are, whispering at the door;
You've never heard them sound so hushed before.
Don't breathe. Don't move. Stay dumb. Hide in your
  blindness.
They're moving closer, someone stumbles, mutters;
Their words and laughter scuffle, and they're gone.
But don't come out just yet; they'll try the lane
And then the greenhouse and back here again.

They must be thinking that you're very clever,
Getting more puzzled as they search all over.
It seems a long time since they went away.
Your legs are stiff, the cold bites through your coat;
The dark damp smell of sand moves in your throat.
It's time to let them know that you're the winner.
Push of the sacks. Uncurl and stretch. That's better!
Out off the shed and call to them: 'I've won!
Here I am! Come and own up I've caught you!'
The darkening garden watches. Nothing stirs.
The bushes hold their breath; the sun is gone.
Yes, here you are. But where are they who sought you?

Vernon Scannell

Late Home

I looked up – the sun had gone down
Though it was there a minute before
And the light had grown terribly thin
And no one played by the shore
Of the lake, now empty, and still;
And I heard the park-keepers shout
As they cycled around the paths . . .
'Closing, closing . . . everyone out . . .'

Then I panicked and started to run,
Leaving all of my friends behind
(I could hear their cries in the bushes –
It was me they were trying to find)
But they had the burn and the minnows,
The rope, the slide, the shrubbery track,
And the trees where a thrush was singing,
And I had the long road back –

The road that led, empty and straight,
Down under the tall grey flats
Where the lights were on, and the tellies,
And old ladies were putting out cats:
I ran past them, without looking round
As though I'd committed a crime:
At six they'd said 'Just half an hour'
And *now* – oh, what was the time?

How could it have gone already?
Something must be, it *must* be, wrong –
I've only just come out – and why
Does getting back take me so long?
I can't be late – or if I am,
It's the fault of the sun or the moon.
When the dentist's takes an eternity,
How are happy things over so soon?

So I stopped and asked, 'Please mister . . .'
And his left wrist came slowly round
And he peered at his watch and shook it
And said 'Blast, it's never been wound.'
But the next man hauled his watch up,
Like a lead sinker on a line,
Clicked open the front, and boomed out,
'Right now, child, it's five to nine'.

There's a great big gap in between
The way things are, the way things seem,
And I dropped down it then, like you do
When you shoot back to life from a dream.
I stood there and muttered 'It can't be –
His watch must be wrong' – then, aghast –
'This time, I'll *really* be for it.
If it isn't a whole two hours fast.'

But I got my legs going again
And ran, gulping in red-hot air,
Through back-streets where no one knew me,
Till I came out in the Town Square.
But when I looked at the shining face
And I heard the cheerful chimes
Of the Town Hall clock – then every hope
Drained away, as it struck nine times.

Two hours late . . . two hours late –
Perhaps they've called out the police
Two hours late . . . who, all in a line,
Are combing the waste ground, piece by piece;
While *they* all stand in our window
Anxious and angry and, when I'm seen,
Ready to frown and shout 'There he is',
'Come here you!', and 'Where's the child been?'

When I come round the corner and see them,
I'll limp, as though I'd a sprain,
Then whimper 'I didn't mean it' and
'I'll never ever go out, again . . .
How can I know that time's up,
When I'm enjoying myself such a lot?
I'm sorry – won't you take me back in?
Are you glad to see me, or not?'

. . . But later in bed, as I lay there
In the extraordinary light –
Filtering through the half-drawn curtain –
Of that silvery spellbound night,
I wondered just what *had* happened
To Time, for three hours in June:
If all of my life is as happy –
Will it all be over as soon?

Brian Lee

A Rich Inheritance

In the early 1970s, the American poet and teacher Kenneth Koch decided that the way to enable his students to get involved with classic poetry, and to enjoy reading it, was to feature these poems as part of their own writing activities. He wrote down his ideas in a book, *Rose, Where Did You Get That Red? – Teaching Great Poetry to Children*. His book was a huge inspiration to me in my early years as a teacher and I began to put my own ideas into practice with the children I taught.

The line 'A sunny pleasure-dome with caves of ice' from *Kubla Khan* led one ten-year-old writer to respond with the following:

> The Ice-Palace
>
> The glistening, sparkling,
> glint of the ice,
> sharp-pointed like shattered glass.
> Statues stiff, cold and silent,
> frozen in ice, fed with hatred,
> their eyes white, hiding a secret of pain.

The Lake Isle of Innisfree by W. B. Yeats is a reflective and gentle poem of longing. Yeats is in the heart of the city and yet he has only to think of Innisfree and he can escape there. Discuss the notion of a place to escape to, whether this be a real or an imaginary one. Children may enjoy composing poems that follow on from Yeats's 'I will arise and go now . . .'

> I will arise and go now to Delmarco,
> where rivers are made of white wine
> and flow like enchanted miracles,
> where the mountains are made of glass
> and shimmer in the moonlight.
>
> I will arise and go now to Delmarco
> where . . .

Tell the story of *The Rime of the Ancient Mariner*, then read Coleridge's description of the icy waters and, later, where the vessel becomes becalmed. Suggest that children write extracts from the ship's log:

> The ship lay becalmed. We sprawled on the decks or hung in the rigging, our throats parched. No wisp of wind disturbed our sails and the sun beat down upon us till the men went mad, raging about the ship, eventually flinging themselves overboard. We can see no hope of release from our suffering.

Similar accounts might be written by members of the 'six hundred' prior to *The Charge of the Light Brigade*, and diary entries could also be written about life in rat-infested Hamelin. Suggest that children focus on one particular incident, such as a wedding feast, and describe how it was disrupted by rats.

*

Children love the sound of the made-up words in Lewis Carroll's *Jabberwocky* and they will enjoy describing the creatures that Carroll writes about:

> The Jabberwock is large and plump. It's like a lion and a crocodile. It has sharp blood-covered claws and nostrils that give out steam. It has a long curly tail, brilliant ears, sly eyes and large dog-like feet. It has a cruel, curious and sort of secretive nature.

Ask children to attempt their own versions of the poem, replacing Carroll's invented words with their own. Challenge older children to keep to the rhyme and syllable patterns.

Langeromer

Twas sangy and the lother gogs
   Did pang and langer in the wase;
All linga were the gangerhogs
   And the honga candase.

Beware the Langerom, my schlen!
   The clanger that shang, the bors that swatch!
Beware the conerhun, and flen
   The zangazing lochershatch!

The main events in narrative verse, such as *The Lady of Shalott* and *The Highwayman*, can be discussed, sequenced and presented as a storyboard. Turn these into board games based on the poems, relating forward or backward moves to events in the poems.

Robert Browning's *The Pied Piper of Hamelin* is an excellent poem to use as a basis for a Literary Project:

* Explore the poem section by section, making sure that everyone understands what is happening.
* Research rats and rat behaviour. Why do rats cause disease?
* List rat expressions and their meanings – to smell a rat, caught like a rat in a trap, rat race, desert rat, like rats leaving a sinking ship . . .
* Write rat raps:

   We're the rats (followed by two beats, then four beats
   on a tambour)
   We're the rats (as above)
   We strut through the kitchen and we sniff for cheese,
   We turn around and we chase our fleas,
   We're the rats . . .
   We're the rats . . .

* Compile an issue of an imaginary newspaper – *The Hamelin Express*. Work in groups and appoint an editor for each paper. Set a non-negotiable deadline.
* Write diary extracts – life in rat-infested Hamelin.
* Describe the Pied Piper.
* Write newspaper reports about:
   (a) the disappearance of the rats
   (b) the kidnapping of the children

CHILDREN DISAPPEAR

Horror as children all over the town of Hamelin disappear. Parents are terribly worried as no one knows where they have gone. An interview with a lame boy who got left behind revealed that they went to a far-off land where silver waterfalls flow and trees produce strange fruit. It can, however, be revealed that the man who took them was:

THE PIED PIPER

Reporter Barry Gilbert will continue with this story in tomorrow's edition.

* Write about the 'joyous land' inside the mountain or make up a travel brochure that would encourage others to visit.
* Prepare wanted posters for the Pied Piper.
* Illustrate lines from the poem or present it as a storyboard.
* Develop a board game based on events in the poem.
* Plan a town guide to Hamelin.
* Dramatize the poem – or parts of it.
* Think about and explore the movement of rats – leaping, scampering, crouching, zigzagging, dodging and pouncing. Develop the idea of working as a pack. Make sequences of movement. Play 'Follow my leader'.
* Find out about the poet Robert Browning and write an author profile.

Ideas for other poems:

Bed in Summer – Robert Louis Stevenson

Many of the poems in Robert Louis Stevenson's *A Child's Garden of Verses* (published in 1885) were written while he was lying ill in bed. The poems were written in the first person and drawn from memories of his own childhood.

Bed in Summer details a child's thoughts on trying to get to sleep in summer when it is light outside. Ask children to think about how they feel in that situation. In which months of the year is the problem particularly noticeable?

Stevenson writes of hearing 'the grown-up people's feet'. Ask children to list other noises that disturb them on light summer evenings – older children playing, someone mowing grass, dogs barking, cars, neighbours talking. These observations could then be featured in a poem about summer evenings.

Alternatively, explore the contrast between winter and summer that Stevenson touches on in verse one of the poem:

> In winter I dress up warm,
> but in summer I just wear shorts.
>
> In winter the nights are cold,
> but in summer they're far too hot.

Can the poem be expressed pictorially? Perhaps a child leaning against the windowsill, looking out into a garden where she can observe all the details that are written about in the poem?

There are many more poems by Robert Louis Stevenson that are suitable for this age group, particularly *Windy Nights, Where Go the Boats?, The Land of Counterpane* and *From a Railway Carriage*. These can all be found in this book.

In a Dark Wood – Anon.

Groups of children can prepare presentations of this poem. They can think about how each line might be spoken and perhaps add background sounds or music. Which group can develop a really spooky interpretation?

Children may also enjoy preparing a series of illustrations to accompany the poem.

Some children will probably wish to write and present their own versions of this traditional poem:

Under the dark, dark ocean there was a dark, dark
shipwreck,
And in that dark, dark shipwreck there was a dark,
dark cabin,
And in that dark, dark cabin there was a dark, dark
locker,
And in that dark, dark locker there was a dark, dark
chest,
And in that dark, dark chest there was . . .
A HUGE AND SLIMY OCTOPUS WAITING TO
GRAB YOU!

From *The Mermaid* and from *The Merman* – Alfred, Lord Tennyson

Children may wish to copy out one or other of these poems and to illustrate their choice. Many will have seen the Walt Disney cartoon film *The Little Mermaid* and be eager to discuss mermaids. Can anyone discover the origin of mermaid legends?

Describe a mermaid or merman. Where might they live: in a cave, a shipwreck, a city under the sea? What would they look like, how would their voices sound, how would their tails feel if you touched them? Write about finding a mermaid in an unexpected location – a museum, a swimming pool, your bathroom, an ornamental lake in the park. What happens?

Children may enjoy writing 'Who would be . . .' poems in the style of these two extracts by Tennyson:

> Who would be
> an explorer brave,
> splashing through
> a huge sea cave,
> only the beam
> from a tiny light,
> to guide him through
> the blackest night.

The Deserted House – Mary Coleridge

Prior to reading this poem, ask the children to talk about

deserted houses that they have come across. Where were they and why were they empty? Were they spooky-looking or did they simply look sad?

Ask children to list the signs that often tell us that a house is deserted. Some children may like to draw, paint or model such a house.

Now let them read the poem. Ask them to choose favourite lines and explain why they like them. Do any of the features mentioned in the poem link in with items on their own lists?

Children might use their lists as a basis for writing. A poem about a deserted house could feature a repetitive phrase which will help to give the poem its rhythm:

> When I passed by the deserted house
> I saw broken windows and a hole in the roof,
> I heard the door creak on its hinges.

> When I passed by the deserted house
> I smelled roses on the overgrown bushes
> and watched birds fly to the eaves.

> When I passed by . . .

The Way Through the Woods – Rudyard Kipling

Consider using this poem for group discussion. Suggest to the groups that they talk and then make notes on the following:

(a) The subject of the poem – how they feel about it

(b) Likes and dislikes, plus reasons why

(c) Any lines or phrases that are puzzling

(d) Any comments on the rhyming pattern

(e) Ideas about when and where the poem might have been written

(f) Any memories of their own that are triggered off by the poem

These initial thoughts can be swapped with another group before being shared as a class.

Groups might then prepare a presentation of the poem, perhaps adding music or other background sounds.

Some children may like to try a piece of writing in response to a memory. Is there somewhere that was once open to everyone but is now closed?

Rudyard Kipling was born in India in 1865 and educated in England. He was a passionate reader and wrote many books, including *Just So Stories* in 1902 and *Puck of Pook's Hill* in 1906. Children may also enjoy reading *The Smuggler's Song* and *If*, both of which are included in this book.

The Listeners – Walter de la Mare

Prior to any reading of this poem, offer children the first two lines and ask them to predict what the poem will be about. Alternatively, photocopy and hand round copies of the poem with the title omitted. Individuals or pairs can read the poem and suggest possible titles. Who comes up with the best title? Whose title is closest to the poet's choice?

What feelings does the poem conjure up? What pictures does it bring to mind? Children may like to draw a response to the poem, looking for clues in the text – moonlight, a traveller, forest, door, turret, etc. Some may wish to pay particular attention to one line or phrase and to sketch this.

Index of First Lines

Index of First Lines

Index of First Lines

Index of Poets

Index of Poets

Acknowledgements

The compiler and publisher would like to thank the following for permission to use copyright material:

W. H. Auden, 'Night Mail' from *Collected Poems*, by permission of Faber and Faber; **Hilaire Belloc**, 'Matilda' from *Complete Verse* by Hilaire Belloc (Copyright © The Estate of Hilaire Belloc 1970) is reproduced by permission of PFD (www.pfd.co.uk) on behalf of the estate of Hilaire Belloc; **Charles Causley**, 'My Mother Saw a Dancing Bear' and 'Colonel Fazackerley', both from *Collected Poems for Children*, Macmillan (2000), by permission of David Higham Associates Limited; **T. S. Eliot**, 'Macavity: The Mystery Cat' from *Old Possum's Book of Practical Cats*, Copyright © 1939 by T. S. Eliot and renewed 1967 by Esme Valerie Eliot, by permission of Faber and Faber; **Eleanor Farjeon**, 'Nine o'Clock Bell!' from *Blackbird Has Spoken*, Macmillan (2000), by permission of David Higham Associates Limited; **Robert Frost**, 'Stopping by Woods on a Snowy Evening' from *The Poetry of Robert Frost*, edited by Edward Connery Lathem, published by Jonathon Cape. Reprinted by permission of the Random House Group Ltd; **Robert Graves**, 'Allie' from *Complete Poems* Volume One, Carcanet Press (1995), by permission of Carcanet Press; **Langston Hughes**, 'Mother to Son' from *Collected Poems of Langston Hughes*, published by Alfred A. Knopf Inc., by permission of David Higham Associates Limited; **Brian Lee**, 'Late Home', by permission of the author; **Walter de la Mare**, 'The Listeners' and 'Silver', both from *The Complete Poems of Walter de la Mare*, Faber and Faber (1975), by permission of the Literary Trustees of Walter de la Mare and the Society of Authors as their representative; **John Masefield**, 'Sea-fever', by permission of the Society of Authors as the Literary Representative of the estate of John Masefield; **Ogden Nash**, 'The Rhinoceros', Copyright © 1933 by Ogden Nash and 'The Dog', Copyright© 1957 by Ogden Nash. Reprinted by permission of Curtis Brown Limited; James Reeves, 'The Sea' from *Complete Poems for Children*, published by Classic Mammoth (2001), by permission of Laura Cecil Literary Agency on behalf of the James Reeves estate; **Vernon Scannell**, 'Hide and Seek', by permission of the author; **Kit Wright**, 'The Magic Box', by permission of the author; **W. B. Yeats**, 'The Lake Isle of Innisfree', by permission of A P Watt Ltd on behalf of Gráinne Yeats.

Every effort has been made to trace the copyright holders, but if any have been inadvertently overlooked then the publishers will be pleased to make the necessary arrangement at the first opportunity.

A Poet a Week

Chosen by Paul Cookson

52 poets and 364 of the best poems of all time.
This contains a huge variety of forms and styles and all
manner of subject matter.

There are ballads, riddles, tongue-twisters, sonnets, shape
poems, raps, narrative verses and haikus; it contains poems
about seasons, festivals, animals, love, war, life and death,
food and football, to name a few. There is also a biography
of each poet at the beginning of his or her week.

An essential book for teachers, but also a joyful
celebration of poets and poetry that readers will return
to again and again.

THE WORKS 4

Every kind of poem on every
topic that you will ever need
for the Literacy Hour

Chosen by Pie Corbett and Gaby Morgan

Divided into 26 alphabetical sections
featuring poems relevant to the Literacy Hour.

The Ark and other creatures, Boys' stuff, Celebrations
and festivals, Dinosaurs, dragons and dodos, Elements,
seasons and the natural world, Friends and families, Girls'
stuff, Home life, Impossible and incredible, Journeys,
Kissing and other things best avoided, Love, death, war
and peace, Monsters, ghouls and ghosts, Nonsense,
Ourselves and others, People and places, Queens, kings and
historical stuff, Rescuing the world, Senses and feelings,
Teachers, Unpleasant things, Viewpoints, Wonder,
X-words and wordplay, Young and old, Zapping aliens.

THE WORKS 5

Every kind of poem, from an alphabet of poets, that you will ever need for the Literacy Hour

Chosen by Paul Cookson

Contains 260 poems from 260 poets:

John Agard, Allan Ahlberg, John Betjeman, Lewis Carroll, Paul Cookson, Emily Dickinson, Carol Ann Duffy, T. S. Eliot, Eleanor Farjeon, John Foster, David Harmer, Seamus Heaney, Jenny Joseph, John Keats, Edward Lear, Roger McGough, Brian Moses, Grace Nichols, Wilfred Owen, Brian Patten, Michael Rosen, William Shakespeare, Kaye Umansky, Oscar Wilde, W. B. Yeats and Benjamin Zephaniah, to name just a handful.

THE WORKS 6

Every kind of poem you will
ever need for assembly.

Chosen by Pie Corbett

From poems about faith, the environment, happiness and
friendship to poems about loss and conflict. There are
poems to celebrate achievement and poems to help us
deal with the times we live in.

A book packed with gems for dipping into
time and time again.

A selected list of titles available from Macmillan Children's Books

The prices shown below are correct at the time of going to press.
However, Macmillan Publishers reserves the right to show new retail prices
on covers, which may differ from those previously advertised.

READ ME FIRST Poems for Younger Readers for Every Day of the Year	978-0-330-41343-5	£6.99
Read Me 1 A Poem for Every Day of the Year	978-0-330-37353-1	£6.99
Read Me 2 A Poem for Every Day of the Year	978-0-330-39132-0	£6.99
The Works Every kind of poem you will ever need for the Literacy Hour	978-0-330-48104-5	£6.99
The Works 2 Poems on every subject and for every occasion	978-0-330-39902-9	£6.99
The Works 3 A Poet a Week	978-0-330-41578-1	£6.99
The Works 4 Poems About Everything	978-0-330-43644-1	£6.99
The Works 5 An Alphabet of Poets	978-0-330-39870-1	£5.99
The Works 6 Poems for Assembly	978-0-330-43439-3	£6.99

All Pan Macmillan titles can be ordered from our website,
www.panmacmillan.com, or from your local bookshop
and are also available by post from:

Bookpost, PO Box 29, Douglas, Isle of Man IM99 1BQ
Credit cards accepted. For details:
Telephone: 01624 677237
Fax: 01624 670923
Email: bookshop@enterprise.net
www.bookpost.co.uk